Radical Elk Hunting Strategies

Secrets of Calling Elk in Close

By Mike Lapinski

Radical Elk Hunting Strategies

Secrets of Calling Elk in Close

By Mike Lapinski

Copyright 1988 by Mike Lapinski

ISBN 0912299-41-X (Hardcover)
ISBN 0912299-42-8 (Softcover)

All Rights Reserved

No part of this publication may be reproduced, stored in a retrieval system, or transmitted in any form or by any means without the prior written permission of the copyright owner or the publisher.

STONEYDALE PRESS PUBLISHING COMPANY
205 Main Street — Drawer B
Stevensville, Montana 59870
Phone: 406-777-2729

TABLE OF CONTENTS

Dedication . . . . Page 6
Prologue — The First Bugle . . . . Page 7
Introduction . . . . Page 9
Chapter 1 — The Rut . . . . Page 11
Chapter 2 — Radical Bull Elk Hunting is Born . . . . Page 21
Chapter 3 — Radical Hunting Techniques . . . . Page 29
Chapter 4 — Hunting the Immature Bull . . . . Page 43
Chapter 5 — Hunting the Mature Bachelor Bull . . . . Page 51
Chapter 6 — Hunting the Herd Bull . . . . Page 59
Chapter 7 — Bugling Equipment and Techniques . . . . Page 69
Chapter 8 — Rifle Hunting During the Elk Rut . . . . Page 79
Chapter 9 — After the Shot Is Made . . . . Page 89
Chapter 10 — Locating Rutting Bulls . . . . Page 99
Chapter 11 — Elk Archery Equipment . . . . Page 107
Chapter 12 — Clothing and Emergency Gear . . . . Page 119
Chapter 13 — Physical Conditioning . . . . Page 129
Chapter 14 — The Condition of Our Western Elk Herds . . . . . . Page 139
Appendix A — State by State Comparison . . . . Page 147
Appendix B — Listing of Best Proven Elk Areas . . . . Page 151
Appendix C — Addresses of State, Federal Agencies . . . . Page 157
Appendix D — Additional Sources of Information . . . . Page 161

Cover Photo: No wild scene more typifies the American wilderness than the bugle of a bull elk.

Dedication

Would that you could live on the fragrance of the earth, or like a plant be sustained by the light.
But since you must kill to eat, and rob the newly born of its mother's milk to quench your thirst, let it be an act of worship. And let your table stand as an altar on which the pure and innocent of the forest and plain are sacrificed for that which is purer and more innocent in man.
When you kill a beast, say to him in your heart, "By the same power that slays you, I too am slain; and I too shall be consumed. For the law that delivered you unto my hands shall deliver me into a mightier hand. For your blood and my blood is nothing more than the sap that feeds the tree of heaven."

From the poem titled,
"The Prophet" by Kahil Gibran

Prologue

Radical Bull Elk Hunting

THE FIRST BUGLE

The stars have all faded in the murky light of predawn. Soon it will be first light on the opening day of elk archery season in Idaho. I've been hiking uphill steadily for an hour to reach a high ridgetop above the North Fork Clearwater River. The air is crisp and vibrant, and frost covers the huckleberry brush. Even in the chill morning air, I'm sweating, and my breath comes in ragged, gulping gasps.

Far off mountain ridges and peaks appear like magic where minutes before there was a black void. Birds begin to flutter through the trees and sing a sweet melody, punctuated by the raucus chatter of red squirrels.

I feel good. Better than that, I feel exhuberant! Work and business pressures are left behind. So is the late payment notice from the bank. At this moment, the disappointments and discouragements of life seem vague and petty. Why? Because It's the first day of elk season!

Still, I want more, and I want it bad. I'd climbed to the top of this high ridge to hear my first elk bugle of the season. I try to control my jumpy nerves. I try to rationalize this intense yearning that I have to hear that wilderness sound. It's no use. I'm an elk bugling junkie looking for a fix.

I fall into a momentary fatigued stupor while staring at the endless forested beauty of the Rocky Mountains. Suddenly, I'm jolted alert! The event that I cherish so dearly is finally happening.

It begins as a low, mournful howl and rises in intensity to a high pitched squeal before dropping off with a hollow grunt. My entire nervous system tingles with that first scorching jolt of adrenalin, and I feel the hot hunter's blood rushing through my veins. The skin on the back of my neck begins to crawl, and my heart is pounding like an Indian drum.

I wait with bated breath. Two minutes, and then three. "Come on," I urge the anonymous bull elk. And then it comes again. This time it's a short bugle, followed by a series of grunts. A sudden gush of adrenalin shoots white-hot through my body. I grab my bow and start forward. If I have my way, that bull has only a few more bugles left in him.

Mike Lapinski
Superior, Montana
August 15, 1988

Introduction

There is no other big game animal that has so completely captured the imagination of America's sportsmen as the bull elk in rut. The tremendous size and beauty of the bull elk is impressive, and it sports a glorious, sweeping set of antlers that are greatly coveted as a trophy.

But more than anything else, it is the heart-pounding excitement and challenge of hunting the bull elk in rut that every fall lures a small army of bowhunters and early season rifle hunters from all over the world to the Rocky Mountains. These men come west with dreams of mighty herd bulls and harems of cows dancing in their heads.

The reality of western elk hunting is that the land is vast and seemingly endless, and the elk are scattered throughout millions of acres of rugged forest terrain. The rutting bulls are there, and there are a lot of them, but they stay hidden in backcountry areas. Add to that the very complex rutting instincts of a bull elk, and you have a situation which can totally confuse a visiting hunter.

I know the feeling. I had the same problems when I first began bowhunting bull elk in rut. I tried the accepted techniques for bringing in rutting bull elk on the run, but my success was limited. I brought in a few bulls, but most were content to merely answer my bugle and stay put.

My frustration led me to a long and intense study of the behavior of the bull elk during the rut. If I was ever going to be successful at hunting rutting elk, I had to understand both why and how they reacted. I traveled to elk preserves and national parks to observe the behavioral patterns of rutting bulls, from the frisky immature bulls to the surly old herd bulls. I finally came to the conclusion that rutting bull elk were far more complex animals than most sportsmen were aware of, and they did not react to a hunter's bugle in the manner that was generally accepted among early season hunters.

As a result, I developed a radical approach to hunting rutting bull elk that contradicts conventional elk bugling methods. My hunting success has skyrocketed, and as I shared my radical philosophy for hunting rutting bull elk with others, their success also increased.

Four years ago, I invited three Wisconsin men to join me on an elk bowhunt in Montana. I had never met the men. My purpose was simply to show a few sportsmen from another part of the country the excitement of western bull elk hunting.

These men knew nothing about elk. They had never hunted them before, and two had never even laid eyes on an elk. In preparation for their hunt, they'd read elk hunting books and listened to every bugling tape that they could get their hands on. On the evening of their arrival, I sat them down at my kitchen table and explained my radical elk hunting philosophy to them. I could see the look of amazement in their eyes as they listened. This was far different from anything that they had read or listened to about hunting rutting bull elk.

I also had a couple of pieces of physical evidence to support my radical philosophy. I'd just killed a big 5X5 bull in Idaho on the first day of archery season the week before, and I'd also killed a dandy 5X6 bull just two days before on the opening day of Montana's elk archery season.

The men from Wisconsin stared bug-eyed at these tremendous trophies. That was enough proof for them! They used my radical hunting approach, hunted hard, and were rewarded with three elk. One of the bulls had a huge 6X7 rack that scored 300 Pope & Young points.

Simply put, my radical elk hunting philosophy recognizes that the bull elk in rut is an animal who performs a rutting ritual. The hunter who understands this mating ritual and uses it to his advantage will greatly improve his chances for success.

This book is dedicated to all early season elk hunters who want to bring home a trophy bull elk. It explains in detail how bull elk act towards each other and how they react to a hunter's bugle. It clears up much of the confusion and misunderstanding about bugling bull elk that will not come in to a hunter's call. Most importantly, this book explains how to successfully hunt the rutting bull elk.

To further help the aspiring elk hunter reach success, this book also covers bugling techniques and hunting equipment, following the blood-trail and field care of game, clothing, emergency precautions, scouting secrets, and concludes with a positive assessment of our precious western elk herds.

And there's more! Appendix A explains which western states have the best elk hunting, which have the most elk, and which states have the most trophy size elk. In addition, Appendix B provides critical state-by-state detail of proven elk producing areas. With an understanding of the radical bull elk hunting philosophy, plus the added bonus of where to find good elk hunting, any sportsman can realistically expect a successful western elk hunt.

Chapter 1

THE RUT

There is no other event in the sporting world that compares with the elk rut. Like a strange metamorphosis, a bull elk changes overnight from a large benign deer into a snorting, frothing, vocal combatant. And if that wasn't enough, this entire intriguing ritual takes place in the breathtaking beauty of the high Rocky Mountain wilderness. In fact, the bugle of the mighty bull elk has come to be recognized as a symbol of everything that is still wild and free.

Actually, a bull elk begins preparing for the upcoming rut back in March when his antlers are shed. Within two weeks, pulpy protrusions appear where days before there were only ugly raw sores. This is also the shedding time for the elk's heavy winter coat, and during these spring months the bull elk hardly looks like the wilderness monarch he will be in a few short months.

Antler growth is rapid, and during this growing period, a bull is very careful to avoid damaging the tender velvet covered shoots. Even bodily injury will cause antlers to become deformed. Such common accidents among elk as broken ribs from a fall, or an injured leg, will cause deformed antler growth during the mending period. In addition, an elk's antlers will be warm to the touch while in the velvet stage and are actually pliable.

By mid-August, antler growth is complete and the tips form out to points. Shortly after, the velvet covering dies. A bull will vigorously rub his antlers against saplings or large bushes to shed the dried velvet.

The result is a spectacular set of long sweeping antlers that are the envy of sportsmen everywhere. A mature bull may have antlers whose main beams exceed five feet in length, and the inside spread between antlers may measure more than four feet. The main beams are a rich chocolate brown in color, and the tines have a peeled-back, ivory-colored hue. Tru-

Antler growth of a bull elk is rapid, and a bull is careful to avoid damaging the tender velvet covered shoots.

ly, these are some of the most spectacular antlers grown by any beast in the world.

All summer long the bulls have preferred the company of their own gender. But with the velvet off their antlers, the bulls become moody and reclusive. Suddenly, they have no use for each other. Older bulls will chase off younger animals from a feeding area, and younger bulls prod and push at each other to show dominance.

The week before the rut is a strange one indeed. Meadows and parks that were recently dotted with both cows and bulls are conspicuously empty. When cows are spotted, they seem preoccupied and nervous. The bulls are nowhere to be seen. They are all back in their own secluded lairs feeling those first confusing, but wonderful, stirrings of rutting lust.

Trees that were carefully rubbed last week to remove the velvet from antlers are now attacked with joyful aggressiveness. The bulls continue to punish trees until they work themselves into a frenzy. They often roll in dust, or their own urine, and they seek out wallows to flounder in the musty waters that contain the scents of other elk.

At first light on a crisp autumn morning, a lonely, high-pitched bugle echoes through the high country.

A bull elk during this pre-rut stage is both absurd and intriguing. A bull may stalk up to a small sapling, drop his antlers to a fighting position, and then begin a silly prancing dance around the tree in mock combat. He'll make false charges and hook his mighty antlers at invisible enemies. He'll drop his head and feed amiably for a few minutes and then suddenly dash around in a wide circle kicking up his heels and shaking his antlers at some unseen foe.

With each passing day, the powerful male hormones are flowing through the bull's system with dramatically increasing frequency. Those wonderfully strange first mating urges that the bull had experienced a week ago rapidly evolve into pangs of lust that threaten to consume his entire mind and body. And in the end, they do.

In every drainage the scenerio is the same. At first light on a crisp early autumn morning, a lonely, high-pitched wail echoes through the high country like the cry of a wilderness ghost. A few minutes later another bugle sounds from a distant ridge, followed by an answering call from a small meadow. Then another bull bugles, and another and another until the squealing challenges of bull elk rise to a crescendo. It is the dawn of the rut.

Early in the rut, bull elk sometimes do not bellow out the classic three-note bugle. Instead, they emit a hollow sounding, throaty grunt, commonly called a "euck" (E-O-O-K!), because that's exactly what it sounds like. In addition to bugling and eucking, a bull will also growl and hiss, especially when angered.

It is very difficult to tell the size of a bull elk from the intensity or tone of his bugle. I've seen some massive bulls who did little more than grunt, while others had a tinny, musical bugle usually associated with younger bulls. However, I have been able to generally tell if a bull is a mature or immature animal. An immature bull, say a three year old four-point, will usually lack the intensity and volume of an older bull. Also, a bull with a hoarse, frog-like bugle will almost always be an older bull.

An experience that I had in western Montana several years ago typifies the unusual rutting sounds that bull elk occasionally make. That particular morning, the elk were not bugling. The only thing I heard was a nasal braying like a mule, which I guessed came from a raven up towards the head of a draw. The closer I got, the louder the raven got. Finally, I heard a hollow tone in the call and recognized it to be a bull elk's raspy grunt. That was the strangest sound that I've ever heard come from a bull elk, and the experience taught me to pay attention to any loud sound during the elk rut.

Sometimes, it is only a matter of days from when the bulls shed the velvet from their antlers to when they begin rutting. Five years ago, my hunting partner Jim Monzie, and I were glassing a secluded drainage in central Idaho that held a half dozen bulls. One of the bulls was a magnificent animal with a huge set of antlers.

Some bull elk have unusual bugles, and a hunter should pay attention to any unusual sound during the rut.

The problem was that it was just three days before archery season began, but the bulls were still in full velvet. We didn't have much hope that the bulls would be in the rut by opening day, but in those three days, every bull in that draw had rubbed the velvet from his antlers. We were greeted in the pre-dawn twilight of opening morning by a chorus of bugling elk.

There is also a period of time very early in the rut when many of the bulls have begun bugling, but not herding cows. You usually see this during the last week in August or the first week in September in the high country. Several times I've spotted a mature bull elk tearing up trees and bugling at one end of a meadow while several uninterested cows fed a hundred yards away and totally ignored the bull.

During those early days of the rut, an immature bull may be seen with a small harem of cows until a mature bull arrives and chases him off. Last fall I spotted a young five-point bull with four cows. I also spottted a huge six-point bull 400 yards away in a creek bottom. For two days the big bull spent most of his time raking his antlers on the brush and sparring with saplings.

One morning while I was photographing the small herd bull, the big six-point bull showed up. Moments before, the young bull was acting like the supreme lord and master of his harem, but he sheepishly trotted off when the big bull came stomping in his direction. Obviously, the younger bull

Early in the rut, mature bulls may bugle, but not yet gather a herd of cows.

A herd bull will gather up as many cows as he can, and he's constantly on the alert to rout any rivals.

had come into full rut a few days before the mature bull.

When the elk are in full rut, it is important to recognize that there is a pecking order consisting of three types of bulls. First comes the mature herd bull. Next in the pecking order comes the frustrated mature bachelor bull, followed by the immature four-point or spike bull. It is critical to understand this social structure of bull elk during the rut because each of these three types of bull elk can be successfully hunted when you understand what type of bull you are dealing with.

Surprisingly, the herd bull will not always be the animal with the biggest rack of antlers, though he is usually an older mature bull who is very aggressive. Last fall I watched a big six-point bull continually put the run on two bachelor bulls that had antlers more impressive than his.

A herd bull will gather up as many cows as he can, and he'll run himself ragged constantly chasing away other bulls and rounding up wayward cows. Some harems have exceeded 30 cows, no doubt keeping the herd bull plenty busy. It is amusing to note that during all this frenzied rutting activity, the cows seem to have a very disinterested attitude.

A cow elk will come into her estrus cycle once every 28 days, beginning in late August. If she is not impregnated during her first estrus cycle, she will come in heat again late in the rut. Of course, not all cows in a harem will be in heat at the same time. The bull keeps them all together, biding his time until each cow comes into estrus.

Wayward cows are dealt with harshly by the herd bull. I was quietly trailing a herd bull with a half dozen cows last September during a photography session, when the herd bull suddenly stopped and looked off to his right. The bull acted very agitated, but I could not see another bull who might be coming in to challenge him.

The herd bull charged off in that direction until a cow suddenly jumped up and scampered back to the herd, looking very much chastised. The herd bull followed close behind her all the way back with his long neck extended like a big snake and his nose stuck up in the air. That cow had wandered off and bedded down, and the bull obviously did not appreciate her independent thinking.

Bull elk are totally consumed by the rut, and they eat very little during this period. The big herd bulls especially show a dramatic weight loss of up to 15% due to lack of food and the hectic routine of mating, rounding up cows, and chasing off intruding bulls. The fat reserve that they had built up over the summer sustains them. As a result, many older bulls have a difficult time surviving the harsh western winter because they have no fat reserve to carry them through the lean winter months when deep snow covers the ground. Winter kills are a common result.

A bull elk's main purpose in life is to mate, and the purpose of his glorious rack of antlers is to insure that the strongest mature bulls in their prime will pass on their seed. However, actual fights between bulls are uncommon. Usually, a lesser herd bull will retreat from a mature challenger,

Wayward cows with minds of their own are dealt with harshly by the herd bull.

and a bachelor bull will move away from the aggressive charge of a herd bull.

Most of the fighting occurs between immature bulls who are experiencing those first wonderful, but confusing, pangs of the rut. Friendly pushing matches and clacking of antlers together is common among younger bulls. Even mature bachelor bulls usually avoid combat.

The time when a vicious fight between bulls occurs is when a frustrated mature bachelor bull does not retreat from the routing charge of a herd bull. One time, I watched a big six-point herd bull three times put the run on a mature bachelor bull that was every bit as impressive in body and antler size. The first time, the bachelor bull trotted off. The second time he stomped off, and the third he stood his ground.

Until then, I'd watched a few harmless pushing matches between lesser bulls, and I half expected the same thing this time. Instead, I watched a short, intense confrontation that was both brutal and eventually mortal.

The herd bull came at the bachelor bull in a crouched run with his neck extended and hair on end. The challenger arrogantly raised his snout, bared his teeth, and hissed. The herd bull slowed when he was about 15 feet away, and for a moment I thought it might end up as another simple pushing match.

The herd bull's ears laid back, and the bachelor bull's ears did the same. I'd been around animals long enough to know what that meant! The animals stood glaring at each other for a moment, and in a blur they'd

Vicious fights occur when a frustrated bachelor bull does not retreat from the routing charge of a herd bull.

crashed head on into each other with a loud "Crack!" I was standing about 40 yards away, and I swear that I could feel the ground shake from the tremendous impact.

For a few seconds the massive bulls strained mightily at each other, but then the bachelor bull began skidding backwards from the sheer brute force of the herd bull. They spun around twice, and the herd bull succeeded in knocking the challenger off his feet. While the bachelor bull was still down, the herd bull twice viciously rammed his dagger-like antlers into the other animal's side just in front of the hindquarters. The bachelor bull regained his feet and fled, limping badly.

I'll never forget the sight of that victorious herd bull standing there, head down, shaking his mighty antlers at the vanquished challenger. From that day on, the lame bachelor bull kept to himself in a thicket and bugled only occassionally. I later learned that rangers had found a mature six-point bull dead in the same area that winter, and I'm sure that it was the same bachelor bull who was injured too badly to survive the rigors of winter.

Usually, by mid-October the rut has run its course. A few bulls may still bugle once in a while, but the harems have dispersed, and the intense rivalry between bulls has ended. To complete this awesome wilderness cycle, bulls once again seek out each other's company and spend the rest of the winter in a lonely fraternity. But the biological time clock is already ticking away. Antlers will shed, new ones will grow, and come fall the bulls will once again feel the fire in their loins.

I discovered that when two rutting bulls did get together, combat was rare. (Photo courtesy Wyoming Travel Commission)

Chapter 2

RADICAL ELK CALLING IS BORN

Back in 1970 when I first began bowhunting for elk, the accepted theory for hunting rutting bulls went something like this: A rutting bull elk was itching for a fight, and if you could fool a bull into believing you were an elk, he'd come right in. Consequently, most bowhunters felt that the key to successful elk hunting was to perfectly simulate a bull's bugle. Hit that right note and any bull would come in.

Few bulls were killed by archers in those days, and just about everyone, including myself, had an inferiority complex about their bugling ability. I was able to get the bulls to answer my bugle, and occasionally one would come in. But for every elk that came in to my calling, there were a dozen that came in only part way or not at all.

Searching for Answers

I began to notice serious discrepancies between the way rutting elk were supposed to react, and the way they actually did during the hunt. My great love for the sport of bowhunting elk and my greater frustration with my lack of success drove me to search for a better understanding of the rutting cycle of the bull elk.

I took a two week mid-September trip to Yellowstone National Park, supposedly to photograph bugling bull elk. But the real reason for my trip was to spend time among bull elk in a controlled atmosphere where I could possibly gain some understanding of the elk rut.

Perfect Bugle Theory Discounted

That first morning in the Park, I came upon a secluded meadow where five bull elk were screaming at each other. The elk were evenly spaced about 300 yards apart. I sat with camera in hand eagerly awaiting a confrontation. Nothing! The bulls continued to bugle, but they all seemed content to stay in their own area. You couldn't ask for bugling any more genuine than this, yet there were no sudden charges or vicious fights.

Bull Elk Rarely Fought

Even more interesting was my discovery that when two bulls did get together, combat was rare. During my entire stay, I witnessed only two minor pushing matches. The afternoon of my first day in the Park, I watched two mature bachelor bulls move towards each other along a lodgepole ridge, and I thought for sure that a battle would result. Those two bulls stood nose-to-nose and bugled insults at each other for five minutes. They each found a sapling and tore it apart, they shook their antlers at each other, and then they began amiably feeding not more than 20 yards apart!

I was dumbfounded! Here were frustrated rutting bull elk within point-blank goring range of each other, yet there was no fight to the death! By the end of that first day I was totally confused about the rutting cycle of the bull elk. However, I was confident of one thing. Bull elk in rut did not react like most hunters were led to believe, and if I was to be successful hunting them, I had to radically change my hunting technique.

During my stay in Yellowstone I observed almost 100 rutting bull elk, and I closely studied their reactions to the bugling of other bulls and to my own calling. I watched how they interrelated with each other, and I paid close attention to what types of situations created confrontations.

Rutting Bulls Perform A Ritual

I came to the conclusion that bull elk in rut performed something of a mating ritual. Totally consumed by the fires of lust, a bull bugled to all the world around him how tough and capable he was. He tore up trees and brush and shook his antlers at everything and anything in his domain. Performing this little ritual left the bull feeling justified. He had no great desire to engage in a potentially dangerous battle with every other bull elk in the woods, and consequently a bull in rut did not go out of his way to confront another bugling elk.

I watched various bulls perform this identical ritual time after time until I was confident that I'd discovered the key to understanding the bull elk in rut. Sometimes the bulls did their thing alone, while at other times two bulls performed this ritual within sight of each other.

There were serious discrepencies between the way rutting bull elk were supposed to act, and the way they actually did act.

I came to the conclusion that bull elk in rut performed something of a mating ritual.

A rutting bull elk usually reacts violently when another bull moves into his domain.

Radical Elk Hunting Is Born

I understood how bull elk reacted during the rut, but I still did not have a good idea of how to use this knowledge to my advantage. An incident between two bull elk that occurred on the next to last day of my stay at Yellowstone provided the key which ultimately led to my radical philosophy of hunting rutting bull elk. I'd been listening to three bulls bugle at each other in the timber beside a small stream, and all three animals seemed content to bugle out their challenges and leave it at that. Presently, one of the bulls began to move towards the creek, but in so doing, he came within 50 yards of one of the other bulls.

When that bull realized that another rutting elk had penetrated his domain, he reacted violently. He charged forward and screamed insults at the other bull. He tore up the brush and pawed at the ground. After the trespassing bull had passed by, the other bull stalked back to the thicket he'd been staying in.

Finally, I had an idea for bringing a bull in to bow range. I would move in and confront a bull elk in his own domain. I tried this idea out on two other bulls on my last day in the park. Both times, I sneaked in until I could get no closer without being seen, and then I bugled. The reactions of the bulls in both cases were instant and nerve-shattering. I was immediately confronted by an angry bull elk at close range who was out to prove that he would not be intimidated by this sudden intruder in his domain.

The First Successful Test

I returned from Yellowstone National Park with a good idea of how a bull elk in rut reacted. I also had an idea of how to get a rutting bull into bow range that was a radical departure from conventional elk hunting methods. My next plan was to head for the north Idaho backcountry and move in and confront the first bull that I heard bugle.

My chance came the first morning out when a bull bugled from a ridge about 500 yards away. I bugled back, and the bull immediately answered. Three times we bugled back and forth. I quit bugling and moved quickly in the direction of the bull. Twice more the elk bugled while I was moving forward, and that helped me stay in the right general direction.

I stopped for a moment to catch my breath, and the bull bugled from the other side of a large alder thicket about 80 yards away. I slipped forward until I was on the other side of the thicket, and I guessed that the bull was about 40 yards away. With trembling hands I raised the elk bugle and challenged him.

There was a deathly silence for a minute and then the bull responded with a furious bugle. The bull raked his antlers against the alders, and his hooves pounded on the forest floor. The elk was going through his combat routine, and I took that opportunity to slip forward another 15 yards.

I kneeled behind a hemlock sapling and bugled. Then I picked up a stick and vigorously rubbed it up and down on some brush to simulate another bull's antlers raking the brush. The bull came forward and began punishing another alder bush not more than 15 yards away. I could see the bull's antlers above the brush and his vague outline through the brush, but there was no chance for a shot.

I quickly nocked an arrow and smashed the brush with a stick to answer his challenge. That did it! The next thing I knew, the bull was coming around the alder thicket on a path that would pass no more than 10 yards away from my position.

His huge antlers moved ominously forward, and I came to full draw a moment before his huge head appeared in the small opening. I forced myself to ignore his mighty rack and placed the sight pin a foot behind his shoulder and low. The arrow zipped forward and buried fletch deep in the elk's ribcage. The startled bull charged off, but stopped about 40 yards away just out of sight.

There was an eerie silence in the forest. I sat violently trembling with excitement and worrying about my shot placement. Had I hit him in the right place? Had the arrow gone in deep enough? Then I heard a strange noise. It sounded like a man clearing his throat. Next, a cough came from the area where the bull was standing. Then another cough, and I guessed that the bull was coughing to clear the blood that was fast filling his lungs.

Suddenly there was a tremendous crash followed by silence. My heart was pounding wildly as I cautiously advanced. As I moved along the blood trail, I found the broken arrow shaft covered with blood lying on the ground. I stepped around a small stand of trees and found the bull lying on his back in a small clump of alder brush. He had a large non-typical, five point rack that made the record book.

Radical Hunting Success Over The Years

Over the years, I've killed 16 elk with bow and arrow, and 14 of those were bulls that were taken as a result of my radical approach to hunting rutting bull elk. Shortly after I began using this aggressive, confrontational elk hunting approach, I met Jim Monzie, a frustrated bowhunter who was looking for some answers. After I'd explained my philosophy of hunting rutting bull elk to Jim, he promptly went out and killed a dandy six-point bull which made the record book. Jim has killed two more bulls with bow and arrow and is sold on the radical approach.

Wisconsin resident Bob Mussey is another bowhunter friend of mine who is sold on the radical method of hunting rutting bull elk. Bob knew next to nothing about elk hunting when I invited him to join me on a bowhunt in Montana five years ago, but he followed my instructions and he has taken home three elk in four bowhunting trips to Montana and Idaho. Bob's last elk was a nice five-point bull that he confronted and killed at 20 yards in central Idaho.

No Guarantees For Success

Of course, a hunter who uses the radical method of hunting rutting bull elk is not guaranteed a kill every time out. Hunting is an imperfect science, and there are many variables that come into play when a hunter is closing in on a bull. A sudden shift in the wind, or the warning bark of a sharp-eyed cow will usually ruin even the best planned hunt. However, I've averaged one kill for every two bulls that I've gone after. In fact, three of the past four years in Montana I've been able to kill a bull elk on the first day of the season.

Remember, It's Confrontation

The thing to remember when you use the radical elk hunting approach is that you are not trying to lure in the bull. You are actually confronting him in his own domain. You are telling him to put up or shut up, and occassionally a bull who is suddenly confronted at close range will choose to retreat. This is especially common among the younger, insecure bulls.

The best formula for success with rutting bull elk is a radical confrontation.

The result of a successful radical confrontation with a rutting bull elk.

Chapter 3

RADICAL HUNTING TECHNIQUES

A radical elk hunter should be aware of a few more tendencies among rutting bull elk to further improve his chances for success. These tendencies have to do with the timing of the hunter's radical challenge to a bull, and the tendency for a bull in the pre-rut period to be more susceptible to a hunter's challenge.

Timing Is Critical

Of primary concern to a radical hunter is the tendency with some bull elk to break off contact with an adversary after he has bugled out all his frustration and torn up a bunch of trees. Consequently, it is vital to move in quickly on a bull elk that responds to your bugle. Don't spend an hour bugling back and forth with the bull. If he answers you twice, he's interested, and you should be charging forward to create a confrontation at close range.

It is my opinion that a hunter is often running against a time clock when he has a bull elk bugling back at him. When I first began radical bowhunting for elk, several times I spent too long hoping that the bull might come in and save me a lot of trouble. Not only didn't the bulls come in, but by the time I started moving in on an elk, he had performed his rutting ritual and was moving off.

Avoid Waiting For A Bull To Come In

Some of my bowhunting friends are amazed when I tell them that I like to quickly move in and challenge a bull even if he is one of those rut-charged animals who is willing to come in over hundreds of yards to my

A bull elk has a tendency to move off after he has performed his rutting ritual.

bugling. An experience that I had three years ago on the first day of archery season in central Idaho illustrates the problem well.

I'd climbed to the top of a long ridge that first morning so that I could listen for bugling elk in the drainage below. I heard no bugles, so when I had hiked about a mile from my pickup I bugled into a small sub-alpine basin about 500 yards away across a deep draw. Immediately, a bull answered and trotted into a small meadow. He began pacing back and forth, and when I bugled again, he answered and came trotting in my direction.

I had an excellent ambush spot just ahead on my upwind side in a small grassy opening created by an avalanche. It seemed obvious that the bull would follow this opening up to my position because the rest of the steep sidehill was choked with alder brush. I hid behind a bush and nocked an arrow. It was a perfect setup, right?

Wrong! While I crouched behind the bush tensed for the bull to appear in front of me, I was shocked to hear him bugle and begin tearing up the brush about 40 yards behind me. The wind was blowing from me to him, and I'd only taken two steps when the bull suddenly crashed off in the direction he'd come.

The problem with allowing a bull elk to come in, is that you have no control over where he will appear, and chances are 50-50 that he'll come in on the downwind side. Also, he may not pass by the exact little opening that you'd planned on. I've even had bulls walk by me through a brushy

The hunter who hesitates to move in and confront a rutting bull may come up short.

area right next to a perfect opening and then catch my scent from a quartering wind.

I would have preferred that that bull had stayed put and performed his rutting ritual while I quickly crossed the deep draw and confronted him at close range in an area of my choosing. That way, I could have been assured that the bull would come forward on my upwind side, and I would have been fairly certain which opening he would have appeared in.

I prefer the rutting bull to stay put. That way, I have the option to pick the spot where the confrontation will occur.

Early Rut Bulls Are Best

My friend Walt Morkert made me aware of the fact that bull elk early in the rut are more susceptible to the challenge of a hunter. Walt believes that mature trophy size bulls that will soon be tough to hunt herd bulls after they gather a harem of cows, will confront a challenger in the pre-rut days.

Walt noticed this tendency over several years of rifle hunting the early "bugle" seasons in Montana. Walt said that he had no trouble getting into trophy bull elk very early in the rut, but after the big bulls had rounded up some cows, they were not interested in a confrontation.

I have also noticed this tendency in pre-rut bull elk to be susceptible to a radical challenge. While other bowhunters are taking it easy and waiting for the elk rut to reach its peak, I make a special effort in the early days of archery season to challenge bulls that are maybe just beginning to enjoy the first pangs of lust and are eager to act out their rutting ritual. As a consequence, my first day success rate is probably due as much to this fact as to the radical hunting philosophy.

Know What Alerts A Bull To Danger

Another important part of radical elk hunting is recognizing what types of things alert a rutting bull elk to danger. In the order of their importance, a bull relies on his nose, eyes, and ears to detect danger.

Human Scent

A bull elk can be totally oblivious to the world around him as he tears at a small sapling. He is so engrossed in his rutting ritual that you might think that nothing could phase his rut-crazed performance. But if one tiny whiff of human scent should carry to his super-sensitive nose, that raging bull elk will scamper into the nearest thicket like a whitetail deer.

I always move in on an elk from the downwind side. And if the elk happens to be on my downwind side, I'll advance in a wide circle and make sure the wind is in my face when I move in to confront the bull. The wind is particularly critical for the bowhunter because he is often very close to the bull when he makes his challenge, and a slight shift in the wind could ruin a perfect hunt. Rifle hunters, on the other hand, can get away with a little more because they don't have to get in so close before a killing shot is made.

Being Seen

A bull also relies heavily on his eyes to detect danger, and a hunter who is caught in the open will usually scare away the bull who spots him. Elk

A bull relies heavily on his eyesight to detect danger. The bowhunter who is caught in the open will usually scare the bull away.

look for movement or objects which are unnatural in their environment. A bull elk who catches a camouflaged bowhunter in the open may not know exactly what he's looking at, but he knows it's not another bull elk. That's unnatural, and he reacts with both suspicion and alarm. Only once in my elk hunting career has there been an exception.

I was after a big bull one morning in northern Idaho, and I was rounding a ridge which ran into a large fern glade. The last time I'd heard the bull bugle, I had pinpointed his position to be right in that meadow. I was surprised when I heard him bugle at the head of the basin a half mile away. Figuring that he had retreated, I charged into the meadow and spotted the bull standing about 100 yards away on the other side.

I cringed and slowly backtracked out of sight. I had no other bright ideas, so I bugled. I was amazed to hear the bull bugle back, and when I peeked over the brush, he was coming in my direction. A sudden shift in the wind sent the bull galloping away across the meadow and into the timber. I later discovered that it was another bull that I'd heard bugle in the head of the draw.

Other than the above exception, every bull that has spotted me quickly retreated. That's why it is very important when you move in to set up a challenge to avoid being seen by the bull. That's not always an easy chore. especially when the elk is located in open lodgepole forest.

I use great care to avoid detection when I get within a 100 yards of a rutting bull. I move forward in short bursts across open areas, and when I

Bull elk that are just beginning to rut have a tendency to be more susceptible to a radical challenge.

Choose your radical challenge site carefully to take full advantage of the wind and cover.

Noise is not a problem when hunting elk. They are big animals, and they make a lot of noise when they move.

stop, it's always behind shielding cover. If I know I'm getting close to the bull, but have not pinpointed him, I may stop for a few minutes to wait for him to bugle, and sometimes I might locate him from the loud commotion he makes while raking his antlers.

Noise Is Not A Problem

Elk are big animals and they make a lot of noise when they move through the forest. A half dozen elk weighing more than 600 pounds each make a lot of stomping, snapping, cracking noises. Consequently, when an elk hears a hunter advancing, he may be curious, but rarely will he be alarmed. Besides, a bull who hears a bugle from a short distance away expects to hear some loud noise from the challenging bull's direction. I often stomp my feet and snap brush when I'm challenging a bull in close to simulate the movement noises of a challenging bull.

This fact is beneficial for the challenging bowhunter who must quickly cover several hundred yards to set up a challenge with a rutting bull before the animal moves off. Save the pussy-footing for whitetail hunting. When you move in on a rutting bull elk, do it fast and don't worry about stepping over every twig in the forest.

Choose Your Challenge Site Carefully

A lot of the success from a radical challenge will depend on where the hunter chooses his ambush site. After you locate the bull, quickly study the area and decide which path or opening the bull will most likely move through when he comes forward to confront you. Then move behind a suitable bush or tree on the downwind side.

After a little practice, it will be easy to tell at a glance which openings the bull will use. I look over the terrain and pick out which path or opening that would be easiest for me to move through, and a bull usually chooses those same openings. I must admit that one time that didn't work too well. I had a bull raking his antlers on one side of a large alder patch, and I was banging the brush on the other side 10 yards away. The obvious route for the bull should have been to come around the bush. Instead, he came right through it! Unfortunately, he saw me while he was still in the thicket, and I could not get a clear shot at him. He quickly departed.

In the brushy elk country where I hunt, I am often able to move to within 50 yards of a rutting bull, and a few times I have set up a challenge within 30 yards of a bull. However, in more open country where your advance may be detected, this will not be possible, and you will have to set up farther back.

My hunting partner, Jim Monzie, doesn't like to move in too close to a rutting bull elk before he sets up a challenge. Jim always stay back about 70 yards even if there is enough cover to move in further. Jim feels that there is too much potential for being smelled or spotted by the bull, or by cows who might be loitering in the area. Jim might have a point there, because I've sure had a lot of promising elk encounters ruined by some sharp-eyed cow.

Be Prepared For Action

It is needless and dangerous to move in on a rutting bull elk over rough terrain with an arrow nocked in your bowstring. However, as soon as you pick your ambush site, nock an arrow and be prepared for immediate action. Twice, I've had bulls come forward immediately after I bugled a challenge from a short distance away. If I hadn't had an arrow already nocked, I probably would not have been ready when those bulls came by.

Short Shots Are Common

Short, deadly shots are common when a bull elk responds to a radical challenge. Jim Monzie has killed two of his three bulls from less than 15 yards away. Most of my shots have been in the 15 yard range, and I've never shot a bull elk any farther away than 30 yards. I took that "long" shot because it was herd bull surrounded by cows, and I dared not move

Short, deadly shots are common when you confront a bull. Jim Monzie has killed two of his bulls from a range of less than 15 yards.

in any closer. In fact, it was one of my most remarkable elk hunting experiences because a cow elk was suspiciously eyeing me less than 15 yards away while I slowly drew back and released the lethal shaft. If she had barked a warning, the hunt would have ended otherwise.

All aspects of hunting rutting bull elk are exciting, but there is something very special about a close range encounter with a rut-crazed bull elk. It is an awesome experience to be positioned in such a way that a snorting, red-eyed bull will pass by almost close enough to touch his rump. It is an adrenalin-charged, nerve-shattering experience that permanently hooks a bowhunter in this fantastic sport of challenging rutting bulls up close. How close? Jim's last bull was shot at a range of eight yards, and mine was shot at five yards. Talk about excitement!

Keep Calm!

The one drawback to a close encounter with a bull elk is that it can be very unnerving. A huge bull that bugles out a furious challenge from 10 yards away on the other side of a bush will cause a bowhunter to almost jump out of his boots! I take a lot of deep breaths to calm my nerves when things start getting hectic and intense. I also use a lot of negative logic. Even when a kill seems eminent, I keep telling myself that something will probably go wrong so there's no use getting excited, which is a definite possibility.

Bowhunters who use sights should be aware that quick shooting is often required when confronting a bull at close range.

Quick Shots

Bowhunters who use sights should be aware that quick shooting is often required when confronting a bull at close range. When a bull moves forward, his long legs will quickly take him past you, and if you are not ready for it, the chance of a lifetime may be missed. This is a big problem when hunting in brushy country.

I constantly watch the bull's antlers or listen for hoofbeats — anything to tip me off that he's coming forward. When a bull approaches the opening where a killing shot can be made, it is important to come to full draw and be ready to release the arrow as soon as the bull's chest comes into the opening. I've had several successful radical elk encounters during which the bull passed through a small opening only two or three feet wide in an area of thick cover. If I had not been at full draw and ready to release the arrow, the elk would have been through the meager shooting lane before I could have drawn my bow.

Why Hunters Fail With Rutting Bulls

One of the most bewildering things about hunting rutting bull elk is their unpredictability. One bull might confront a radical challenge from a hunter until the last moment and then move off, while another bull might come right in. An then there is the bull that begins to move away immediately when a hunter challenges him.

The hunter usually blames himself. He figures that he didn't bugle correctly, or he didn't set up right, or he didn't fool the bull. The real reason for the supposed unpredictable nature of certain bull elk is that there are three distinct types of rutting bull elk.

Chapter 1 noted that rutting bulls fall into one of three categories. There is the immature bull who lacks the confidence to face a challenge, and the mature bachelor bull who is capable of servicing a harem and facing a challenge. Last, there is the herd bull who is more interested in moving his harem away from a challenging bull.

The hunter who recognizes the fact that there are three types of rutting bulls, each one with different tendencies, will not be constantly baffled by an elk's seemingly unpredictable actions. There are ways to determine which type of bull has answered your call, and there are hunting methods that will prove successful on the immature, bachelor, or herd bull.

There is no guarantee for success when hunting rutting bull elk. The most promising hunt can quickly end with the swirling of the wind.

I bugled and immediately an answer floated back.

Chapter 4

HUNTING THE IMMATURE BULL

An immature bull is usually a four-point or small five-point elk, usually called a raghorn, of about three years in age. While a mature bull elk will weigh 800 pounds or more, a raghorn will not weigh much more than 600 pounds. A spike bull does not have the physical or biological makeup to participate actively in the rut. Spike bulls often hang out with the cows, and a herd bull will occasionally even tolerate the presence of a spike bull along the outskirts of his harem.

The third year is the first season when a young bull is capable of mating, and a raghorn is filled with a wonderfully confusing drive to procreate. Unfortunately, the bigger bulls have all the cows, and those first few clumsy attempts by a raghorn bull to move in and help himself to one little cow from among a large harem will not be appreciated by the surly herd bull.

The raghorn quickly learns that the herd bull does not share his wealth of cows. After a few frightening and often painful encounters with various herd bulls, the immature bull is often tentative and sometimes downright scared of any further confrontations.

Last fall, I watched a young five-point bull continually move in on a herd bull's cows. The raghorn would stay about 300 yards away, out of the herd bull's view, watching for a wayward cow. Whenever a cow wandered away from the others to feed by herself, the raghorn would slowly move in her direction.

When the raghorn got close enough to the cow to start getting ideas, the herd bull, who'd been aware all along of the raghorn's presence, would turn and start walking in his direction. The herd bull would come at the raghorn in a low crouch with neck extended, snout upthrust, and hackles up. Whereupon the raghorn would retreat.

This happened several times during the first two days while I was

An immature bull is usually a four-point or small five-point.

photographing the elk, and with each confrontation, the herd bull got a little closer before the raghorn departed. The raghorn became more brazen and began bugling a challenge at the herd bull. Twice, when the herd bull took several threatening steps in his direction, the raghorn pawed the ground, dropped his puny antlers into a fighting position and then shook his rack at the bull. He performed a little prancing mock battle no more than 40 yards from the herd bull, who'd by then become ferocious.

The raghorn was playing a game. It was fun to play big, bad, rutting bull in front of all those cows. I knew that it would end soon. And from the looks, hisses, and growls coming from that, by now, demon-possessed herd bull, it would end permanently if he had his way.

Finally it happened. The raghorn was going through his cute tough-guy routine, when the bull suddenly turned and started after the raghorn in a gallop. The last I saw of the raghorn, he was galloping at full speed over a small open ridge, and the enraged herd bull was only a few feet behind and gaining. They no sooner disappeared when a loud crash sounded and dust flew into the air.

A moment later, the herd bull stalked back over the ridge and joined his harem. I later saw the raghorn, and he looked thoroughly cowed. In fact, whenever he spotted the herd bull after that, he quickly swapped ends and moved away. I would guess that the herd bull finally caught up to the raghorn as soon as they went out of sight, and the herd bull made the raghorn understand that the rut was not a game after all.

This huge herd bull is about to teach a young raghorn that the rut is not a game.

You can understand a raghorn's reluctance to confront a hunter's challenge at close range after he's survived a few experiences like that. He may bugle back at a hunter's call, and even go through the rutting ritual, but when it comes down to a nose-to-nose confrontation, a raghorn that has had the fear of the herd bull put in him will lack confidence.

Consequently, a young bull is responsible for most frustrating bugling encounters that a hunter experiences. The raghorn will respond to a bowhunter's call, and he'll even tear up the brush when the hunter moves in to challenge him, but just when it looks like a killing shot might be possible, the bull retreats.

It's easy to understand why a hunter might think that he did something wrong when everything is going according to plan one minute, but the bull is gone the next. However, raghorn bulls can be hunted successfully if the hunter is aware that it's a raghorn he is moving in on to set up a radical challenge.

Almost half of the bulls that I've killed with bow and arrow were raghorns, usually smaller five-point bulls. I believe that a large part of my success with killing raghorn bull elk is due to the fact that I hunt hard during the early part of the rut when the bulls are just beginning to perform their rutting ritual.

A young bull is responsible for most frustrating bugling encounters because he tends to retreat when things start to get interesting.

During this pre-rut period, a raghorn bull has not yet met with some of the more sobering realities of the rut, namely the unappreciative herd bull. He feels good all over, and he's driven to perform the rutting ritual of bugling, tearing up brush, and rolling in his own urine. He also thoroughly enjoys getting into friendly pushing matches with other young bulls. He's not quite sure why he's doing all of it, but it feels good.

One time I watched four young bulls perform in a high country meadow in central Idaho in late August. All four bulls were prancing around and tearing at brush with their antlers. Two of the bulls would clack antlers and begin pushing at each other while the other two stood by with heads down, ready to join in the fun. The elk would go back to feeding for a few minutes, but before long they'd be back to playing their pre-rut games. This went on for over an hour.

It's difficult to always be able to tell the difference from a bull's distant bugle whether he is an immature or older animal. I once killed a record book herd bull whose bugle was so tinny sounding that I guessed it to be a raghorn or another hunter! However, there are a few guidelines that often reveal the general age of a bull.

A mature bull will occasionally have a high pitched, weak bugle, but most older bulls have a hoarse bugle with high volume. A raghorn bull will rarely have a hoarse bellow like the older bulls. If an answering bugle lacks volume and generally sounds cheap, chances are that it is a young bull. Add to that the fact that a certain bull may be erratic in his answering bugles, and you have a further indication that it's a raghorn. Sometimes, a raghorn or spike may only "euck" instead of bugling.

The hunter who is fairly sure that he is moving in to challenge a young bull should avoid giving the elk the impression that he is a big bad bull. Instead, he wants to give the impression that he is just another young bull who has come forward to play the rutting game. Avoid the deep, big-bull bugle and the frantic beating of brush. If the raghorn is bugling, do the same but keep the volume down and the tone more musical than rasping. Another trick is to answer the bull only with "eucks" or short bugles. Sometimes, I will not even answer a raghorn's bugles or grunts. Instead, I'll just rub a branch against a tree to simulate antlers raking brush.

A raghorn bull flush with the first delirious joys of the rut will often come right in to a radical challenge if he has not had any painful experiences with mature bulls. In fact, the last few raghorn kills that I've made have seemed downright easy due to the eagerness of the young bulls to engage in a little harmless confrontation with another bull.

However. the raghorn bull who has the rut fever bad, but has had a few frightening encounters with herd bulls, will often accept a radical challenge, go through all the bugling and antler raking rituals, but then move off for no apparent reason.The answer is simply that the young bull lost all his nerve at the last moment. That doesn't necessarily mean that

The hunter who is fairly sure that he is moving in on a young bull should tone down his bugling to avoid alarming the animal.

the hunter is defeated. A young bull can still be successfully hunted if the hunter quickly moves forward and creates another radical challenge.

My hunting partner, Jim Monzie, killed a raghorn five-point bull while I was with him three years ago that I found an amazing feat, mainly due to Jim's condition. Just two weeks before Idaho's elk archery season opened, Jim's face was smashed in by a tree that had kicked back while he was logging. Jim spent two weeks in the hospital getting all the tiny splinters of bone removed that once had been his cheekbone, and he had a plastic plate installed to replace the pulverized cheekbone. It didn't look like Jim would be recuperated in time for archery season, but a lot of prayer was put into the situation, and Jim was able to take up the bow and arrow a week into Idaho's archery season.

However, Jim was not able to load up a backpack and set out on those torturous day-long (and usually halfway into the night) backcountry jaunts that he so dearly loves. Instead, he was restricted to hunting close to roads. One evening, we stopped along an old road across from an open sidehill with timber above it.

I bugled and immediately a bugle floated back. A moment later a young bull emerged from the timber. We watched through binoculars as he put on quite a rutting performance. We dropped off the edge of the road, slid down about 1,000 feet of steep mountainside until we splashed, literally, into the creek and then started up the other side.

Our legs were like jelly from the excruciating forced march up the steep sidehill. We heard the bull bugle about 80 yards ahead from a small pocket of timber. Jim bugled, and the young bull charged forward and begun raking his antlers on a large alder bush about 50 yards away.

Both elk and hunters went through the rutting ritual for about five minutes, but then the young bull suddenly trotted off. We slowly advanced and spotted a wildly swishing bush about 40 yards ahead. The raghorn was punishing the bush and bugling, so we did the same. Again he retreated and we followed. But this time he stayed put probably because Jim just "eucked" instead of going through the rutting ritual. So far so good, the bull did not retreat, and Jim slipped in to about 20 yards away.

Jim banged the brush several times and then nocked an arrow. The bull walked around a bush where Jim was hiding, and Jim put an arrow through the elk's lungs from the point blank range of eight yards. The bull trotted off about 20 yards and then stopped and looked back in confusion. He stumbled and caught himself, and then he dropped dead in his tracks.

The best way to hunt a tentative young bull elk is to avoid making too much of a rutting uproar. Duplicate his actions, and keep your bugling soft. If the bull moves off, wait until he bugles once or twice and then move in again. After a few of these harmless confrontations, the raghorn may get his rutting instincts fired up and come forward to meet his challenger. If it looks like he's not going to come forward, try to slip in for

A young bull will often come right in to a radical challenge if he has not had any bad experiences with older bulls.

a shot while he's preoccupied raking his antlers on the brush.

The wind will often determine the success of a prolonged radical confrontation with a young bull. The first time that a hunter moves in, he can make sure that the wind is safely in his face. But with each short retreat by the bull, chances increase that your human scent will be carried to the bull by a swirl of the wind.

Radical hunting for the immature bull elk goes to extremes. In the early part of the rut, a raghorn may come waltzing in almost asking to be killed. Later during the rut, a young bull who has had several close encounters of the herd bull kind may be understandably timid, and it can be tough to get one to accept a challenge. Occasionally, you will encounter an immature bull that continues to retreat after a half dozen confrontations, and it becomes obvious that he will not allow you to get close to him. In this situation, it might be wise to break off contact with that bull and search for a more receptive rutting elk.

A mature bachelor bull will sport an impressive rack of antlers.

Chapter 5

HUNTING THE MATURE BACHELOR BULL

A bachelor bull is a physically mature animal at least four years old that has experienced previous ruts. His antlers size ranges from a large five-point rack at four years of age to a trophy size six-point beyond that age. A bull that I killed in Idaho several years ago was a typical four year old specimen. The bull had a large, symmetrical five-point rack that scored 239 points, just one point short of the Pope & Young minimum of 240 points.

Biologically And Physically Impressive

The bachelor bull is not only an impressive physical specimen, but his body has also developed the mature genes necessary to produce strong offspring. And, of course, he is more than willing to do his part to spread his seed throughout the female elk herd.

Yet for all his physical and biological assets, the bachelor bull has no harem of cows to service. In fact, some bachelor bulls go through the heat of their first and second ruts without getting a chance to satiate their fiery mating urges even once. For whatever reason, certain bachelor bulls are not capable of gathering a harem of cows and then repulsing the challenge of other mature bulls. Even more peculiar is the fact that a bachelor bull left groaning all alone in his rutting agony may actually be bigger in body and antler size than the local herd bull.

Bachelor Bulls Are Frustrated

Given the above physical and mental condition of the average bachelor bull, you can imagine how he might react when a hunter comes forward for a radical challenge. It's bad enough that he can't mate and he's being driven crazy by the fire in his loins. It's bad enough that he was recently embarrassed by the local herd bull. Now some impudent bull has suddenly invaded his domain and dared bugle out a challenge!

My hunting partner, Jim Monzie, encountered such a bull in western Montana in mid-September several years ago. Jim had heard three bulls bugling along a low ridge a half mile away late one evening, so he quickly advanced until he arrived in a small swale below the ridge. Jim bugled and immediately an answering bugle ripped through the chill autumn air from about 60 yards away. He'd unwittingly walked right into the domain of a rut-crazed bull elk.

Jim said that it sounded like there were a dozen elk tearing up the woods in the area where the bull had bugled from. Alder brush flew into the air, dirt spattered against trees and leaves, and Jim heard a furious pounding of hooves. Only one elk was making all that racket, and it was obvious that he did not appreciate Jim's bugling challenge.

Jim moved forward another 20 yards and bugled again. The bull screamed back and started towards him. Jim admitted getting a bit shook up because he missed the bull clean at 20 yards. The bull swapped ends and trotted off about 40 yards, obviously unaware of exactly what had spooked him.

Jim stood shaking with excitement, feverishly thinking of something that might give him another chance at the bull. He bugled again, never expecting the bull to respond. He was shocked to see the bull swap ends and come toward him in a fast walk. This time, Jim's aim was true, and he made a perfect heart shot at 15 yards. The bull stumbled a few steps and collapsed. He was a beautiful six-point which now resides in the Pope & Young record book.

A Radical Challenge Is An Insult

A radical confrontation is more than a challenge to a frustrated bachelor bull. It's an insult! Nothing else has gone well for him lately. He has no harem. He still smarts from his last encounter with the local herd bull. He hasn't eaten much for days. Now some elk has invaded his space! Given this emotional state of mind, it is easy to see why a bachelor bull presents the best opportunity to kill a trophy size elk.

Avoid Waiting For A Bachelor Bull

A bachelor bull is the same animal that will, on occasion, come from a long distance to a hunter's bugle. However, a hunter who has only limited time to hunt may waste his entire hunting trip crouched behind bushes hoping for one of these infrequent occurrences. I spoke to a bowhunter last year who had spent an entire week hunting in an excellent elk rutting drainage in north Idaho, but he went home without an elk.

A frustrated bachelor bull usually reacts violently to a radical challenge by raking brush with his antlers.

This insulted bachelor bull fell victim to my radical challenge.

The man told me that he had anywhere from two to four bulls bugling at him every day, but none of them would come in. He said that twice he had bulls come part way in. One bull had even advanced to within 50 yards and began raking his antlers on trees, but the elk would not come all the way in. The guy thought that he must have been bugling wrong. I didn't have the heart to tell him that if he'd been more aggressive and had set up a radical challenge on any of those bulls, he could have taken home a trophy.

In all my years of bugling elk. I've had only two bull elk who came over a long distance to confront me. One of those bulls came from a distance of about 400 yards, and the other bull came in about 500 yards. The rest were content to bugle out a challenge and stay put. Sure, a few of those bachelor bulls that I quickly moved in on might have come in on their own. But as I mentioned before, a hunter in this situation is often put at a disadvantage because he has no control over where the bull will come in.

An Aggressive Challenge Is Best

A radical challenge to a bachelor bull should be done with much vigor. An immature bull may be intimidated by a hunter's overly aggressive challenge, but a bachelor bull seems to get even more worked up to match the aggressiveness of his adversary. A hunter's first challenging bugle should be loud and clear, followed by a loud grunt at the end. Succeeding bugles should become increasingly hoarse to reflect an elk's growing frustration.

An aggressive challenge works best with a bachelor bull.

I believe that the closer a bowhunter can move in before he challenges a bull, the more aggressive his challenge will appear. If you set up a challenge at 100 yards, the bull may feel threatened, or he may be content to stay where he is and perform his rutting ritual. At that range, he has the option to come in or stay put. But when you challenge him at 30 yards, he can't stay put. He must either come forward or retreat.

Just for fun, let's put a radical challenge in human terms. Suppose you were walking down one side of a city street, when some guy began yelling threats at you from across the street. You may become irritated, and you may even hurl a few threats back. Feeling justified, you continue on your way, feeling smug in the way you told the guy off. You also would not feel particularly threatened as long as the guy stays on his side of the street. Suddenly, the guy is only a few steps behind you hurling threats and insults. If you are like me, you'd feel a mixture of fear and outrage at this sudden intrusion. You have the option of running or turning to face your adversary. That's the scenerio on a city street with men, and that's much the same situation that you put the bachelor bull in when you set up a radical challenge.

Brush Banging Often A Catalyst

Brush banging is often the catalyst that brings a bachelor bull forward during a confrontation. However, a bull does not actually "bang" his antlers against a bush. He finds a small tree or stout bush and rubs his antlers against its trunk. A hunter should try to simulate this action instead of swinging wildly at bushes with a stick. As soon as a bull begins raking his antlers in front of my ambush site, I'll grab a stout limb from the forest floor and rub it against a nearby tree trunk. Make sure you have an arrow nocked and ready when you start banging the brush because a bull is most likely to come forward when he hears it.

Bachelor Bulls Have Classic Bugle

A bachelor bull usually has a clasic three note bugle. It's not too difficult to tell the difference between the often imperfect call of an immature bull and the clear, high pitched bugle of the mature bachelor bull. The problem is that you usually can't tell from a far off bugle if the elk is a bachelor bull or a herd bull.

Bachelor Bull or Herd Bull?

As you move in to set up a radical challenge, there will be indications to further help you decide which type of bull you are about to challenge. If you have moved to within 80 yards of the bull, and you haven't noticed any cows wandering around, it's probably a bachelor bull. Even if you

Try to determine whether it's a bachelor bull or herd bull before you confront the animal. Hunting strategy will depend on which type of bull you expect to encounter.

don't see cows, you can often hear these large, heavy hooved animals stomping and rustling through the forest. Also, a bachelor bull will almost always stand his ground to bugle back a challenge at a hunter, while a herd bull is prone to begin moving his herd away from a rival as soon as he hears a bugle close by.

Not a Sure Thing With a Bachelor Bull

Still, it's not a sure thing when a hunter sets up a radical challenge on a bachelor bull. That bull may have just been roughed up by a herd bull, and he is not interested in another confrontation. In this situation, he may scream his outrage at a challenger in his domain and tear up trees and brush to vent his frustration. Performing this rutting ritual alone may leave the bull feeling justified, and he may not come forward to challenge the intruder.

When a Bachelor Bull Retreats

On occasion, a mature bachelor bull may retreat to avoid a confrontation. Even in this situation, a hunter can be successful by following closely behind and setting up a challenge whenever the bull stops.

I encountered a bull elk last year in Montana that had all the symptoms of a frustrated bachelor bull. However, after 15 minutes of bugling back

A frustrated bachelor offers the best chance for success during the peak of the rut.

and forth at 40 yards and listening to the bull tearing up the brush, I realized that the animal was not going to come forward. I scooted ahead another 20 yards and tried to force the issue, but instead the bull moved off about 100 yards.

I could see the animal as it slowly stalked off, so I followed him until he entered a spruce thicket. I advanced to within 30 yards of the thicket and bugled. The bull raged at this further intrusion and harassment, and he came forward to rout the brazen imp who would not leave him alone. I shot him at about 10 yards, and he dropped after stumbling about 40 yards. He was a nice four year old with a five-point rack.

Best Chance For Success

During the peak of the rut, a frustrated bachelor bull is one of the easiest bulls to bring in with a radical challenge. While the immature bull has become a bit timid by then and is not as vulnerable as he was early in the rut, the bachelor bull is much more prone to come forward to face his challenger as the lustful fires of the rut inflame him. But don't wait on him! Otherwise, you may be waiting until next hunting season!

Chapter 6

HOW TO HUNT THE HERD BULL

The herd bull is usually the most impressive representative of his species — and he knows it. A herd bull has that "John Wayne" swagger that tells you, "I'm the biggest, baddest bull of the woods. And if you don't believe it, try me." He is the supreme lord and master of his harem. He chastises wayward cows, and puts the run, or worse, on lesser bulls foolish enough to challenge him.

When you visit Yellowstone National Park during the September elk rut, you immediately begin seeing big elk. And then you see even bigger elk. There are rut crazed six-point bachelor bulls roaming the high country lodgepole forests and parks in Yellowstone that would be the trophy of a lifetime for most sportsmen. It makes you wonder, "If the bachelor bulls are this big, what do the herd bulls look like?"

When you finally locate a herd bull, he makes you redefine the word "big." In the middle of a secluded meadow stands a monstrous bull elk surrounded by a harem of faithful cows. What an animal! He may tip the scales at 1,000 pounds, but it is not his size that awes you. It is his enormous antlers. Long sweeping main beams arch almost back to his rump, and long wicked-looking tines rise skyward to show off to the world their ivory-colored, dagger-like tips.

Herd Bulls Are Not Always The Largest

Occasionally, a herd bull will not be the most impressive animal in either physical size nor antler size. Due to the scarcity of bigger bulls in a particular area, or his aggressiveness, a smaller herd bull may reign supreme. At least until a truly deserving representative of the species shows up.

The herd bull is usually the most impressive animal in the area — and he knows it.

I know of several five-point herd bulls that have been killed by hunters, but for the most part, a herd bull will be a six-point or bigger. I killed a five-point herd bull a few years back that had a 5x6 rack that didn't even make the record book at 236 points. I believe that this was a situation where it was a very small side drainage, and there were no other big bulls in the area to take over the younger bull's harem.

Herd Bull Is Most Difficult To Hunt

While it is true that a herd bull usually sports the most coveted rack of antlers, it is also true that he is the most difficult rutting elk to kill. He will respond to a hunter's bugle, but very rarely will a herd bull leave his harem to cover several hundred yards of high country terrain to locate the source of a distant bugle. Why should he? He already has what he wants!

Not A Challenge, But A Warning

A herd bull's bugle is not a challenge, as with lesser bulls. It's more of a warning, and the closer a challenging bull gets, the more threatening a herd bull's bugle becomes. I've had herd bulls so angry with me when I'd moved in too close that they actually growled. It's enough to make the hair on the back of your neck stand on end when one of those monstrous herd bulls begins growling and hissing just 20 yards away.

Hunting A Herd Bull Can Be Frustrating

Besides being difficult, hunting a herd bull can also be very frustrating. A good example is a hunt that I had in Montana one evening after a big herd bull. I was in a rough area, with only an hour of shooting light left, so I didn't want to get too far from my pickup. I bugled from a ridge into a long, remote basin, and immediately a bugle ripped through the air only 200 yards away.

I charged forward to set up a radical challenge. I advanced as far as I dared and bugled again. The bull bugled back, but he was still about 200 yards away. He'd moved on me. I had an indication that I was after a herd bull, so I quit bugling and charged forward again.

I began seeing numerous cows casually moving ahead of me, and I knew I was in trouble. I could not get in close to confront the bull and hopefully have him turn to face my challenge. With that many cows milling around and only an hour of light left, I should have broken off contact and returned in the morning. Unfortunately, I caught a glimpse of the herd bull as he sulked along with the cows. He was huge! He was everything I'd always wanted in an elk trophy, and he was barely 100 yards away!

To make a long story short, I charged, ran, walked, crawled, and a few times even rolled, over some of the steepest, brushiest, most blowdown infested terrain that the Lord put on this earth. In one nightmarish hour I'd covered over two miles, and when the light had faded to an uncomfortable murky gloom, that *&%#@$ bull was still 100 yards away and still sulking along with those cows all around him! At that moment, anyone foolish enough to have followed me into that hell-hole could have purchased an entire bowhunting outfit real cheap. I was not only very frustrated, but I also had a long, spooky hike back out of that basin in the dark.

A Herd Bull's Bugle

A herd bull's bugle has the high volume and clear tone of a mature bull elk. An old trophy bull will sometimes have a very hoarse, raspy bugle that identifies it as an older animal. It is almost impossible to identify a herd bull from a bachelor bull by listening to a bugle. Consequently, when a hunter is advancing to set up a radical challenge, he should be alert for any small clue which will tell what type of bull he is about to encounter.

Cows Are A Sure Sign Of A Herd Bull

Cow elk loitering in the area where the bull had bugled from are a sure sign that your quarry is a herd bull. In brushy country, harems tend to be more loosely controlled, and an advancing hunter should not mistake

The herd bull is one of the most difficult animals to kill during the rut.

meandering cows as unattached animals. They are part of the herd bull's harem.

Cow elk serve as the ears, eyes, and nose of the herd bull while he performs his biological duties, I don't have enough fingers or toes to count the number of times that I've had promising hunts ruined by the harsh bark of an unseen sharp-eyed cow. A bowhunter friend of mine, Walt Morkert, related how he'd once penetrated the female defensive formation of a herd bull. Walt had the herd bull enraged and concerned, and he expected the bull to step into the open at any moment.

Walt crouched behind a small spruce tree, arrow nocked, waiting for the big bull to take just a few steps more. At that moment, he had the uncomfortable feeling that something was watching him. Walt told me, "I slowly turned to my left and almost dropped my teeth from my mouth. I was staring defeat in the eye. More accurately, I was staring a big old cow in the eye 10 yards away. She slowly raised her head and turned up her nose. I cringed because I knew what was coming next. The cow barked

A herd bull tends to continue to move away from an advancing hunter.

Loitering cows are a sure sign that your quarry is a herd bull.

Rich LaRocco proves that success is possible with a big herd bull. (Rich LaRocco Photo)

and the entire forest exploded with stampeding elk. I should have shot that cow for revenge!"

Success Is Possible With A Herd Bull

A herd bull is difficult, but not impossible, to hunt successfully. The first thing that a radical hunter must decide as he moves in is whether or not he is about to challenge a herd bull. It is critical to avoid detection and that inevitable cursed warning bark from the milling harem of cows. When a hunter has advanced as close to the cows as he dares, he should bugle a challenge. Usually, a herd bull will return the bugle and move away, but I once had a herd bull come forward immediately to challenge me when his cows were reluctant to leave a prime feeding area. The moral here is to be ready for the unexpected when you close in on the herd bull.

Pressure The Herd Bull

A herd bull may move off only a couple hundred yards to an area where he feels his harem is safe. A hunter should again advance as close as the cows will allow and challenge the bull again. It may take only a few of these challenges before the increasingly agitated bull turns to face his adversary, or it could go on until dusk ends the hunt.

The secret to forcing the herd bull to stop and accept a challenge is to penetrate the natural defense of the cows. A herd bull may shrug off a challenge from an unseen foe somewhere beyond his harem. However, a challenging bugle that suddenly comes from the midst of his cows will cause the herd bull to immediately confront his adversary.

Four years ago, I was guiding a bowhunter from Wisconsin, and we were after a herd bull who was also being pestered by two lesser bulls. We not only had to deal with the herd bull and his milling cows, but now we also had to be careful to avoid the two frustrated bachelor bulls.

We followed the herd bull for about a half mile, but we could not get any closer than 80 yards because the cows were in the way. One time, I thought our hunt had surely ended when one of the bachelor bulls responded to my bugle. He was a decent five-point, and he walked right up to the other side of a large bush we were hiding behind. He could not quite decide what we were, and I whispered to my client that it was up to him to take the sure kill 15 yards in front of him or try some more for the herd bull. If it was my bow, my hunt, and my money, I know which choice I would have made, but my trembling client chose to try for the herd bull. Luckily, the bachelor bull just snorted and trotted off without alarming the other elk.

The harem of cows moved onto a low, sharp ridge below us, and the animals wandered off both sides of it, feeding. What luck! We had an unobstructed route along the crest of the ridge to penetrate the herd. We scooted down the steep slope on our butts until we got to the ridge and then ran forward in a low crouch until we were even with the cows. I quickly bugled, and the herd bull exploded! He bugled and charged onto the brow of the ridge and stood 30 yards away looking at us.

"Shoot!" I whispered. My client, gasping for breath from the murderous pace, raised up and shot. The arrow went high and would have passed two feet over the bull's back, but it hit a limb halfway there and deflected downwards into the bull's chest! The bull went 50 yards and piled up. His rack had six points on one side and seven on the other. He was a tremendous trophy and later was measured at 290 Pope & Young points. I guess when you're hot, you're hot!

Natural Obstacles Help A Hunter

A herd bull that continues to move away can sometimes be made to

I was able to penetrate the natural defenses of the cows to successfully confront this herd bull.

stop and challenge a hunter when the herd encounters a natural obstacle. A blind canyon, a swift river, an open logging area, or even a busy forest road are natural obstacles that an elk herd may balk at crossing.

The herd may not swap ends and head directly back at you, but it may turn and skirt along the edge of the obstruction. If you know about, or see, a potential natural obstacle up ahead, be ready to close in quickly to challenge the irritated herd bull while the cows mill around deciding their next move.

A Hunter Must Know When To Quit

An elk can walk casually over the rough Rocky Mountain terrain faster than a man on the run. A herd bull and his harem who stay on the move are difficult to keep up with, and there comes a point during one of these chases when a hunter must admit that it would be fruitless to continue chasing after the swift moving elk. You might be smart to break off contact with a retreating herd bull and seek out another bugling elk who might offer a better chance for success.

A radical challenge on a herd bull requires a lot of time, and you sometimes must cover a mile or more while following the herd. For this reason, I avoid going after a herd bull during the evening hunt. If things

A natural obstacle such as the rocky basin in the background will sometimes stop a herd bull's retreat.

don't work out with the herd bull, you may find yourself a long way from camp or vehicle in the dark. Even if you are successful, it is a very difficult chore to field dress an animal the size of an elk in the dark. The long, arduous hunt for the herd bull is one of the most challenging and exciting hunts during the rut, but it is better done in the morning.

Chapter 7

BUGLING EQUIPMENT AND TECHNIQUES

Back in 1972, I had a golden opportunity to get rich. I'd read a short article written by a southern gentleman who'd taken an elk hunting trip to Colorado. This man heard an elk bugle, and he discovered that he was able to duplicate the elk's call by using one of his mouth diaphram calls used for hunting turkeys back home.

My friend Dick Wadsworth, a turkey hunter himself, followed up on this idea. He demonstrated his elk bugle to me by blowing a turkey mouth diaphram through a grunt tube. I was astounded! Not only by its clarity and volume, but also by its exact replica of a real elk's call. I realized that this was the dawning of an elk calling revolution.

That's when I made my big mistake. Instead of marketing an exciting new brand of elk call, I was short-sighted enough to spend all my creative time killing elk with it. This is a tongue-in-cheek history of the advent of the superior commercial elk calls currently available. I don't even have the market cornered on hard luck stories concerning the mouth diagram elk bugle. I've heard essentially the same tear-jerking story from several other prominent elk hunters who had read the same article back in 1972.

Excellent Commercial Calls Are Available

Elk calling has changed dramatically from the 1970's when the only commercial calls offered were flute-like whistles that did not produce a very good replica of a bull elk's bugle. Today, excellent commercial elk diaphram mouth calls and reed-type bugles, com-

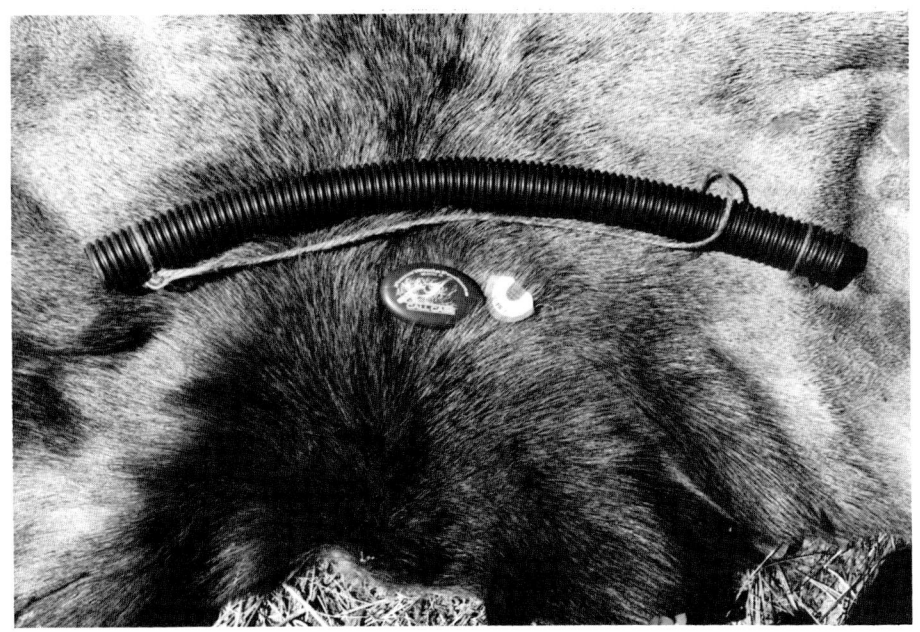

Modern elk bugles evolved from turkey diaphram calls.

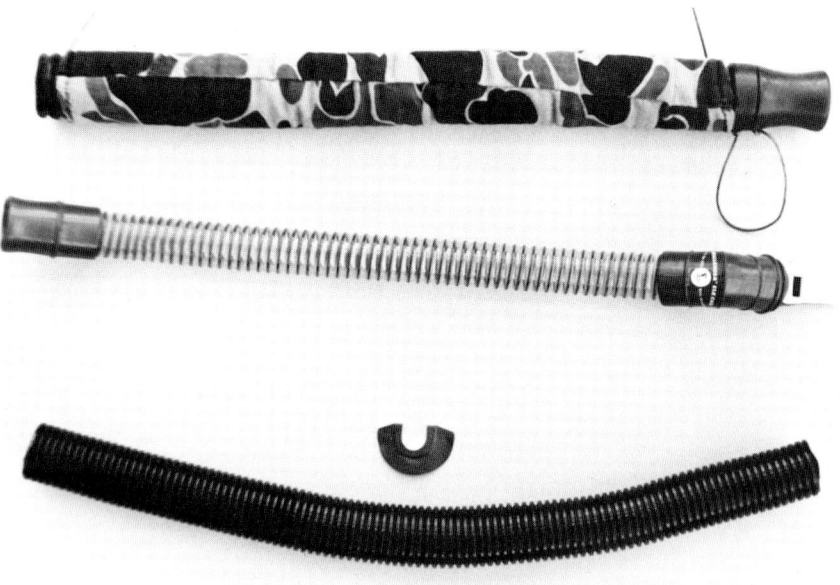

Several excellent commercial elk calls are available today.

plete with instruction tapes, are available through major mail order firms. Any nonresident hunter who has never even heard a real elk bugle can practice at home and come out west assured that he is fully capable of sounding like a rutting bull elk.

A few years back, I offered a free hunt to three Wisconsin bowhunters to join me in western Montana to hunt rutting bull elk with bow and arrow. I cautioned the men to purchase elk calls and instruction tapes and practice their calling during the off-season. When they joined me in September, I was amazed at how proficient they'd become at bugling. I dared not admit it to them, but one of those guys used an elk diaphram better than I ever could. They received their due reward for their diligence and took home three elk.

Reed-Type Elk Bugle

The reed-type elk bugle is a good call for a guy who doesn't have the time or desire to master the sometimes tricky mouth diaphram. In addition, some folks who have full denture plates are not able to use a mouth diaphram, and the reed-type call is an excellent alternative.

The reed-type elk call has a permanent reed installed in a mouthpiece which is connected to a hollow grunt tube. A hunter blows into the call to create a reasonably good elk bugle. There are a few drawbacks to this call. It must be used at full volume to create the high-pitched sound necessary to simulate an elk's bugle. A hunter cannot slowly increase his breath flow to create the low-high-low pitch like a bull elk does. The reed produces a loud, duck-like "Quaaack!" at low volume and should be avoided, especially at close range. Consequently, the reed-type elk bugle is a good, high volume call for long range, but a hunter must be careful with it when bugling in close to a bull.

Mouth Diaphram Elk Call

A mouth diaphram elk call is nothing more than a turkey diaphram that has "Elk Call" stamped on it. A hunter places the diaphram against the roof of his mouth and holds it in place with the sides of his tongue. He then blows air between his tongue and the diaphram. The rush of air causes the diaphram to vibrate and produce a high-pitched squeal.

That squeal in itself is impressive enough to catch the attention of most bull elk. However, when you blow it through a grunt tube to give it a hollow resonance and then add a few more cosmetic sounds, you can produce an elk bugle that is impossible to tell the

The reed-type elk bugle is a good call for the guy who can't master the diaphram call.

difference between it and the real thing. I begin my elk bugle by making a short. low-pitched "W-O-O" sound like a bull does. Then I go into the high pitched diaphram squeal and end with a loud, hollow "G-R-U-F-F" like a real bull does.

A hunter can be fooled by a distant commercial elk bugle because he only hears the high squeal. However, at closer range, you can avoid quite a bit of embarrassment by listening close for the grunt at the end of a bugle. A bull elk will always have a loud, gutteral grunt at the end of his bugle, but a man-made call will not. Except for mine. Consequently, I have the amusing experience every fall of breaking the hearts of several excited bowhunters who mistake my call for the real thing.

Creating A "Euck"

Another benefit of the mouth diaphram elk call is that it can also produce the other sounds of an elk's bugle. An elk often ends a long high-pitched bugle with a series of eucks or he may simply euck without bugling. A mouth diaphram creates a prefect euck. On the other hand, it is difficult to produce a euck with a reed-type call.

The diaphram elk bugle makes an elk call that is very difficult to distinguish from the real thing.

My Choice Of Mouth Diaphrams

Back in 1972, there were no commercial elk bugling diaphrams available, so we used Penns Woods turkey calls. These calls came in a three-pack consisting of a single, double, and triple reed diaphram, along with a coin purse type of holder. The price was a fraction of what an "Official Elk Diaphram Call" costs today, and I still use these simple turkey calls with obvious success.

I especially like the various reeds in the turkey calls because they can be used to vary the volume and tone of a bugle to fit the situation. If I want to sound like a big bad bull, I use the triple diaphram, but if I want to fool a timid immature bull into thinking that I'm just another raghorn, I'll use the single reed diaphram which produces a more high-pitched musical bugle.

The Cow Call

Besides its dreaded warning bark, a cow elk also emits a loud bird-like call of greeting or communication. This loud, high-pitched musical chirp is a signal of safety among the members of an elk herd. Calf elk also emit a nasal, bird-like chirp much lower in volume than a full grown cow's call.

Using Cow Calls On Bulls

A hunter can use a cow call effectively when hunting rutting bull elk. My friend Dick Wadsworth has lured in several immature and bachelor bulls by switching to a cow call when the elk hesitated to come in to a bugle. These types of bulls hear that cow call and are drawn forward by the hope of stealing away a wayward cow. A herd bull can also occasionally be fooled by a cow call. A hunter who sets up a radical challenge should bugle and then give one or two cow calls. The herd bull may be fooled into thinking that his adversary has taken over some of his cows, and he'll come forward to get them back.

Using Cow Calls On Cows

A hunter can also bring in other cow elk with a cow call. Last year during the opening minutes of Montana's archery season, I heard the nasal chirp of a calf elk about 60 yards away. I guessed that there would be a cow with the calf, so I called to her. A minute later, a loud chirp sounded from the direction of the calf's call.

I called twice more, and the cow answered once. Five minutes later, I heard a loud snap of a twig. Hoof beats and rustling noises

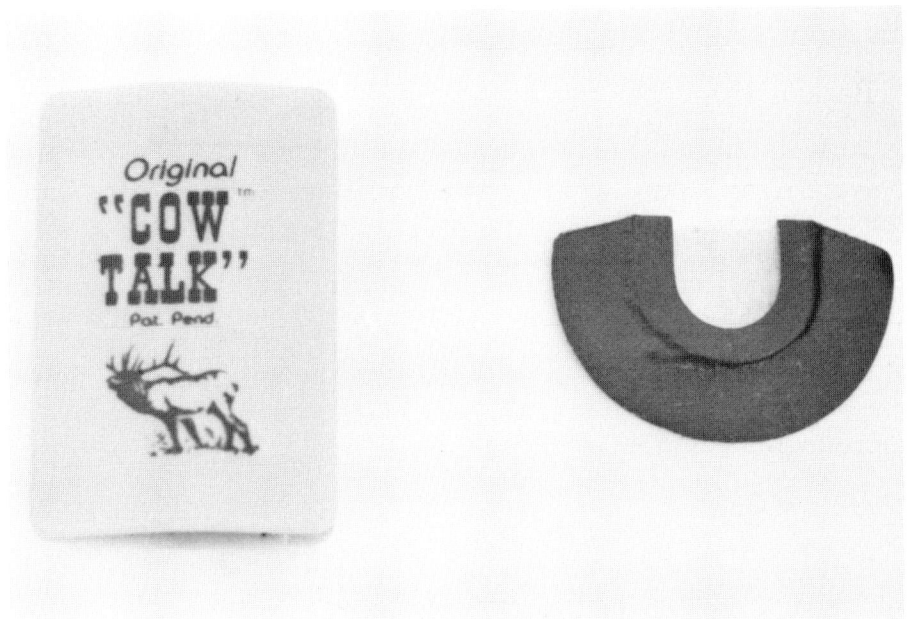

A cow call creates a loud bird-like chirp which serves as a greeting among cow elk.

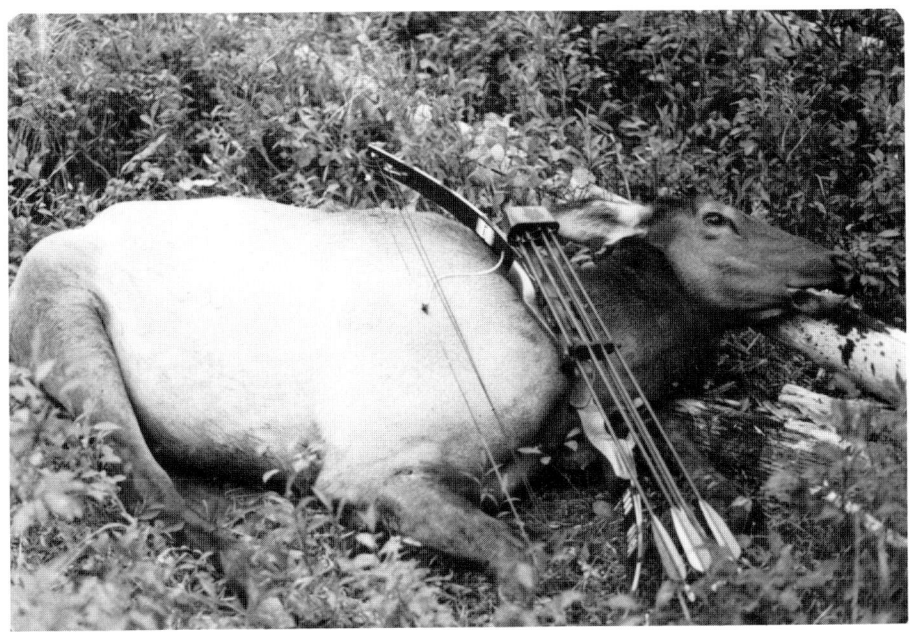

This cow was brought into bow range by using a cow call.

came from that direction, and then I saw the cow slowly feeding in my direction. She was only 20 yards away, with the calf right behind her when she chirped again, but I was too close to chance a return call. I had no intention of shooting the cow, so I waited until she got 15 yards away and stepped into the open. The startled cow almost trampled her bewildered calf when she spun around and crashed away.

Cow calls are offered commercially in the form of an individual call, or as a cow-call mouth diaphram. Both types work well, but I simply use the same mouth diaphram that I bugle bulls with, and it works well.

There Is No "Best" Elk Call

There are numerous manufacturers of both reed-type and mouth diaphram elk calls who advertise their product as a sure-fire tool to bring in a rutting bull elk. Guess what? They're all correct. Other than a few obviously poor calls, all the major manufacturers of elk calls produce acceptable products.

However, don't be misled by some of the more aggressive advertising that claims a certain call will produce that magical "Pied Piper" effect. Bull elk do not float in euphorically to the mystical tone of a particular elk call. Hopefully, by now the reader will be aware that there is a whole lot more to successful bull elk hunting than simply hitting the right tone on a bugle.

There Is No "Right" Bugle Note

This misconception that there is a "right" note to hit that will bring in a bull elk on the run is a common error in reasoning among many hunters today. I spoke with a bowhunter last fall who told me that he had a bull raking its antlers on a tree 100 yards away. The guy said, "I must have hit the right note with my bugle a couple of times because the bull came forward twice more. The last time he was only 50 yards away banging the brush with his antlers, but I just couldn't hit that right tone again." That guy has never killed an elk with his bow and arrow, and he will never know how easy it would have been to kill that bull elk with a radical challenge.

Voice Calling

Some experienced early season elk hunters use their voice through a grunt tube to make an excellent replica of a bull elk's bugle. Not many sportsmen can do this type of bugling, but those who do are very good at it. I'm not one of them. I have never been

A calf elk emits a soft nasal chirp.

able to come up with the rich, full sound that other voice buglers come up with.

My friend Walt Morkert is the best that I've ever heard at voice bugling. Surprisingly, Walt does not blow out. Instead, he sucks breath in, and I would defy anyone to tell his bugle from the real thing. The one big drawback to voice bugling is that it lacks volume. Beyond 200 yards, it becomes a faint murmur, while a mouth diaghram in the same situation can be heard clearly a quarter mile away.

Some voice buglers compensate for this lack of volume by using a reed-type bugle for long distance calling, but when they move in on a bull, they snap off the mouthpiece and use their voice through the grunt tube to further challenge a bull. Also, just about anyone can become proficient enough to "euck" using their voice through a grunt tube.

There is a whole lot more to successful bull elk hunting than simply hitting the right note on a bugle. (Rich LaRocco Photo)

Chapter 8

RIFLE HUNTING DURING THE ELK RUT

The elk rut is commonly associated with bowhunting, but in recent years western states have been moving their rifle hunting seasons forward to the first part of October when bull elk are still rutting. In addition, some states allow certain backcountry areas to be set aside for early "bugler" seasons for rifle hunters.

Montana and Idaho are two good examples of that. Montana's general rifle hunting season for elk begins in late October after the rut has ended. However, in the vast Bob Marshall Wilderness area, rifle season begins in mid-September, and rifle hunters primarily pursue bugling bull elk. State officials say that its the only way to trim the elk herd in that backcountry because much of it is snowed in by rifle season. Whatever the reason, the early bugle season in the Bob Marshall is one of the most exciting rifle hunts in the West.

Idaho also offers several backcountry early season rifle hunts. I've hunted the early season in the Mallard-Larkin Roadless Area of northern Idaho, and it was one of the most pleasurable and exciting hunts that I've ever been on. In addition to high powered rifle hunts during the elk rut, many western states now offer a black powder hunting season that coincides with or occurs immediately after the early archery season. If you are a rifle hunter, you can find an early season elk hunt in just about every western state. Give it a try, and you'll experience the intense excitement that bowhunters have enjoyed for years.

Exciting Rifle Hunting

Rifle hunting for elk in the vast western forests can sometimes make you feel like you're looking for a needle in a haystack. The land is rough and seemingly endless, and elk are not found everywhere. However, when you add to the above situation the fact that the bulls are bugling out their location, you end up with a spectacularly excitement-charged hunt.

My hunting friend, Kelly Johnston, phoned me the evening before opening day of rifle season in Idaho. Kelly knew that I'd been bowhunting there the previous week, and he wondered if I'd heard any bulls bugling. Idaho's rifle season began the first week in October, a bit late for the rut, but Kelly hoped that I might have encountered some late rutting elk.

The week previous I'd killed a bull with my bow in a small basin where the elk had started rutting late. Even though the rut had ended, and the cows had dispersed, some of the bulls were still bugling. The first morning of rifle season, Kelly and I drove to the area where I'd been hunting. It was a two hour hike from the road to the spot where the bulls had been bugling, so Kelly began hiking long before daybreak. Kelly told me later that he had some doubts about heading into a strange area in the dark. Then a bull bugled and Kelly quickly forgot his misgivings.

At first light, four bulls were bugling somewhere in the dense brushy forest across a draw some 500 yards away. Kelly quickly advanced and found himself surrounded by the bulls. What a delicious dilemma! Kelly decided to shoot the first legal bull he encountered. He was moving along a small ridge towards a bull that was bugling every 10 minutes. Suddenly, an elk eucked to his left. Kelly jumped and turned to find a suspicious spike bull watching him less than 30 yards away. Kelly dropped the elk in its tracks.

Kelly is now sold on early season rifle hunting for bull elk in rut. He told me, "I've always enjoyed rifle hunting for elk, but hunting them while they're bugling puts an added dimension of excitement into the hunt. I've never enjoyed an elk hunt like I did that one with four bulls announcing their presence close by."

A Rifle Hunter Must Move In

Obviously, a rifle hunter does not have to move in as close to a rutting bull elk as a bowhunter does. A bull elk rutting 200 yards away is still a long way from being killed by a bowhunter, but for the rifle hunter it only takes one clear shot at that distance for the hunt to be a success. The problem is that bull elk usually don't rut in the middle of open parks where a rifle hunter can easily knock one down. Instead, bulls like the security and seclusion of heavy thickets during the rut.

The rifle hunter who stands on a ridge and bugles all day at rutting bull elk, hoping to bring one in or draw one into rifle range, will end up being as disappointed as the bowhunter who makes that same mistake. The rifle hunter has the advantage of the high powered rifle, but he still must move in close enough to get a clear shot at a rutting bull elk.

A rifle hunter who encounters a bugling bull elk should quickly advance

Kelly Johnston with the spike bull that he moved in on. (Kelly Johnston Photo)

The rifle hunter who moves in on a rutting bull in dense cover has an excellent chance to make a kill.

to confront the animal. My friend Walt Morkert usually moves in to about 100 yards of a rutting bull before he bugles. Walt waits about five minutes before he advances any further, hoping that the bull will come forward or expose himself. However, Walt is careful to not get too close to a bull when he is rifle hunting to avoid being scented, and he'll take any reasonable shot he gets.

That's one of the great advantages of rifle hunting over bowhunting when pursuing rutting bulls. The bowhunter must often move in very close before he can get a good shot, thereby exposing himself to a sharp-eyed cow or the whims of a fickle wind. The rifle hunter, on the other hand, needs only to see the bull clearly to bring it down.

Walt told me that he's had rutting bulls move in on him during rifle season, and he's made the mistake of allowing them to keep coming when they were in easy rifle range. Suddenly, the bulls were gone as quickly as a spooked whitetail when the wind shifted. Walt's last rifle-killed bull was not given the chance to wind him. Walt said, "I had the bull interested in a confrontation, and he was moving in my direction through an old logged over area. He was right out in the open, so I couldn't see taking any chances. I dropped him when he was 60 yards away."

Hesitate And Someone Else Will Score

One of the dangers of hesitation when rifle hunting during the rut is that someone else may slip in and kill your bull while you are procrastinating.

A radical challenge works well for the rifle hunter.

Walt's hunting partner, Jess James, recounted to me a situation where a huge bull elk had eucked several times from a small thicket. Jess moved in to about 100 yards away, but he hesitated going any farther because he was afraid that the bull might see or smell him. Instead, he decided to euck at the bull and hopefully draw him out of his lair.

Hunter and elk eucked back and forth for a half hour with no improvement in the situation. Jess was contemplating moving in on the bull when a tremendous explosion ripped through the forest. Another hunter had heard the bull eucking, and the man had slipped in and killed the rutting elk at a range of 60 yards. Jess said, "Next time I won't wait. I'll take my chances with the wind."

Scent Danger Not As Great

A bowhunter must be very careful to have the wind in his face because his radical challenge will usually be set up at close range. On the other hand, a rifle hunter can often get away with a poor wind condition. I've moved in on bull elk through a cross wind, and I didn't have any trouble because at 100 yards, you don't have to worry about a swirling wind carrying your scent to the bull.

A rifle hunter can often use the long range capability of his weapon to successfully hunt rutting bull elk.

The great advantage of the rifle hunter is that he can drop his bull at longer range before the animal gets a chance to wind him.

One time I even scored on a rutting bull with the wind at my back. I was on a low ridge, and a bull was bugling somewhere below me about 150 yards away. I could not afford the luxury of circling the bull because I had seen two other hunters a while back moving up the same small draw where the bull was bugling. It was fairly open lodgepole forest, and I guessed that I would be able to see the bull before my scent got to him, but I had to move fast.

I quickly slipped forward, scooting from bush to bush to avoid detection. I finally caught sight of the bull about 80 yards away. He had seen the two hunters moving up the draw and was peering intently down at them when I squeezed the trigger. I'm sure if I had waited much longer that bull would have winded me, but my plan to move in quickly, ready to shoot, had paid off.

Long Range Hunting

A rifle hunter can often use the long range capability of his high powered rifle to successfully hunt rutting bull elk. Two years ago I met four hunters from Seattle, Washington, while I was scouting in the Clearwater River drainage of northern Idaho for the upcoming hunting season. These men had adapted their hunting techniques and firearms to successfully hunt rutting bull elk.

The upper Clearwater country is extremely brushy, and some sidehills have walls of brush 10 feet high. The elk can be found bugling and eucking on these brushy sidehills at the opening of rifle season, but a hunter has a difficult time moving through this brush jungle. Consequently, a bull elk usually smells, hears, or sees the hunter and is gone before a shot can be made.

These Washington hunters tried bucking the brush at first, but quickly recognized the futility of it. Instead, they split into pairs and each team climbed the ridge opposite the hillside and sat on rock outcrops listening intently for rutting bulls and glassing the brushy sidehill.

When a bull was located, a rangefinder was used to calculate the exact distance, and then only one man did the shooting while the other glassed the bull and coached the shooter. Once a bull was down, one of the men went across to find it while the other man helped him locate the trophy in the brush jungle by using hand signals. These men had their rifles sighted in to drop only 12 inches at 400 yards, and they did a lot of long range practice shooting at home. They almost always took home four bulls after a week of patiently hunting just that one brushy sidehill.

Choosing The Best Calibre For Elk

There are five calibres that are favorites among western elk hunters. They are the .270 Winchester, 7mm Remington Magnum, 30-06 Spr-

The .300 Winchester magnum is an excellent elk gun.

ingfield, .300 Winchester Magnum, and .338 Winchester Magnum. As I said, they are the favorites, but there is also a host of other lesser known calibres that are also used successfully for elk.

The .270 Winchester

Some hunters consider the .270 to be too light for elk. They may have a point, but the credentials of the .270 in certain situations cannot be denied. Also, the .270 is a favorite of many sportsmen who want to do some long range antelope and mule deer hunting while on their elk hunt.

The .270 is an adequate elk calibre because its oversize case contains enough powder to push a 150 grain bullet into the 3,000 fps range. Its retained energy at 400 yards is nearly 1,200 ft/lbs, which is plenty to ruin any bull's day with a well placed shot. The .270 was the famous Jack O'Connor's favorite elk rifle, and for the skilled hunter it still has its place today. The big drawback of the .270 is that its top bullet weight is only 150 grains. Consequently, hunters looking for a specialized elk rifle will probably pass on the .270 and opt for a calibre that offers a heavier bullet and more retained energy.

The 7mm Remington Magnum

Some gunsmith must have heard the complaint about the .270 because the 7mm Magnum was invented with a slightly larger case that held enough extra powder to push a 175 grain bullet faster than the .270 could move its lighter bullet. That means the 175 grain bullet from the 7mm Magnum retains nearly 1,500 ft/lbs of energy at 400 yards. Bullet drop is only about 30 inches at 400 yards. Minimal bullet drop, moderate recoil, and adequate knock down power at extreme range make the 7mm Magnum an excellent elk gun.

The 30-06 Springfield

The 30-06 has had a long and deserved history that we don't need to go into here. Suffice to say that it is by far the most popular all-around big game rifle calibre. For the hunter who will use the same rifle to hunt everything from elk all the way down to groundhogs, the 30-06 can't be beat with its wide variety of bullet weights ranging from the hefty 220 grain slug to the tiny 110 grain bullet.

Loaded with its most popular 180 grain elk hunting bullet, the 30-06 retains about 1,350 ft/lbs of energy at 400 yards, and its bullet drop at that range is 35 inches. That's plenty to knock a bull off his feet! The 30-06 is a proven elk killer, and thousands of elk are killed with this calibre every year.

The .300 Winchester Magnum

Serious sportsmen who do a lot of elk hunting often choose the .300 Magnum. This mighty calibre pushes a 180 grain bullet at 2,000 fps at 400 yards with 1500 ft/lbs of energy. With the .300 magnum in hand. a hunter need never wonder if his bullet will have enough authority if it must

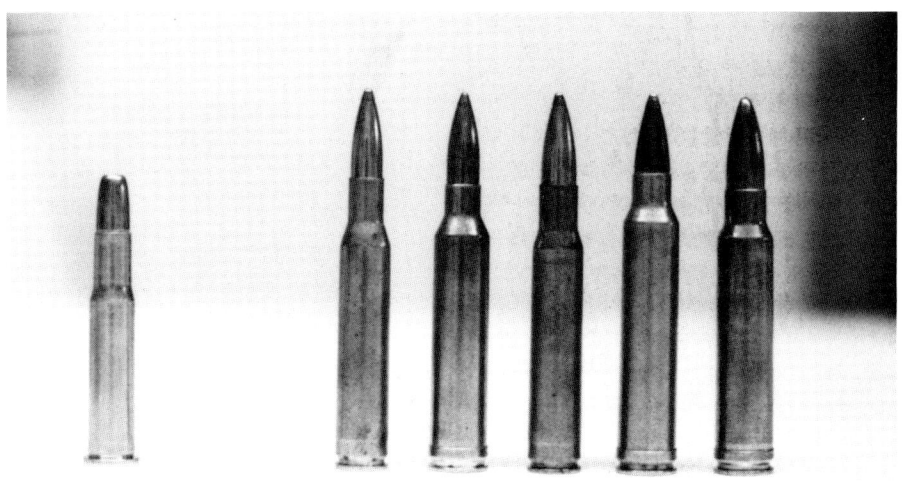

The top five elk hunting cartridges on the right dwarf a 30-30 cartridge.

A retreating young bull may eventually get his rutting instincts fired up after several radical challenges and stand his ground.

reach 500 yards across a canyon.

A hunter looking strictly for an elk gun couldn't find a better calibre than the .300 Magnum. That is, if he isn't bothered by recoil. The .300 Magnum lives up to its designation as a "magnum" at both ends of the rifle. The .300 is usually a heavy rifle to lessen recoil, and some hunters don't like to carry a 12 pound rifle around all day.

The .338 Winchester Magnum

The .338 is an elk gun. Besides the occasional moose, it isn't much good for anything else in the lower 48 states. Bullet weights begin at 200 grains and end at 300 grains. In fact, ballistics tables show that the .338 has more power than is needed to kill an elk.

Even so, the .338 Magnum has become popular among some serious elk hunters. There are some good reasons for choosing the .338 Magnum for elk. First, its tremendous knockdown power even at extreme range cannot be denied. Enthusiasts note that a less-than-perfect shot on a bull elk at 400 yards with a .338 will still knock the animal down. Secondly, bullet stability is very good, and the velocity of the heavy 200 grain bullet will not drop off as quickly as that of a lighter bullet traveling at the same speed. Also, the heavier bullet is not as susceptible to wind drift.

Chapter 9

AFTER THE SHOT IS MADE

(Bloodtrailing, Field Dressing, Packing)

The hunt is not over after a bull elk has been hit, and it certainly cannot be called successful until the mortally wounded animal is found. In fact, a hunt cannot be fully appreciated as an accomplishment until a downed bull is located, field dressed, and then packed out of the woods.

Bloodtrailing

It is easy to find a bull elk after it has been shot. Simply shoot the critter through the heart and it will practically drop in its tracks, and it doesn't matter whether a bullet or arrow is used. I shot my last bow-killed bull elk at eight yards, and I rammed the arrow through the elk's heart. The bull stumbled a few steps and went down for good. Sounds simple, doesn't it?

But what happens when an elk doesn't drop immediately, and you can hear the brute crashing off through the forest for five minutes? A lung or liver shot will kill an elk within a few minutes, but that bull may have galloped through 200 yards of very difficult terrain before it dropped. In this situation, a hunter must patiently follow the bloodtrail until his trophy is found.

Early season bowhunters and rifle hunters especially have a problem following a mortally wounded elk. There is not yet tracking snow to make the trailing job easy. In fact, the brush will often still have its leaves, making visual sighting impossible. In addition, the frost burnt leaves that have fallen to the ground are bright red and blood spots are tough to see on them.

It can't be called a successful hunt until the trophy is found.

Patience Is The Key

Patience is the key to following the bloodtrail. The hunter who gets too excited and goes chasing blindly through the forest in the direction the elk fled has very little chance of catching up to the elk. As a result of his blind charge through the forest, he may not be able to find the place where the elk was standing when it was shot. There may be an excellent blood trail to follow, but the impatient hunter who can't find the spot where the hit was made is on the verge of turning his dream hunt into a nightmare.

Immediately after a hit is made, mark the spot where you are standing, and then walk over to the exact spot where the elk was standing and mark it. I carry some fluorescent orange ribbon in my breast pocket, and I tie a piece of this highly visible plastic ribbon high up on a tree limb or bush. While you are doing this keep track of the elk's movement with your ears and eyes as best you can. It's very helpful to have a general idea of which direction the elk fled if the bloodtrail gets spotty.

Wait A Half Hour

Wait a half hour for the elk to run off, bed down, and bleed out. An elk often doesn't know what happened when he is shot, and he just wants to get out of the area. After he has run 100 yards, and he begins to feel sick, he will bed down and quickly bleed to death. But if you push him, a bull

Patience is the key to following the bloodtrail. Don't push a mortally wounded animal into a thicket where tracking is impossible.

can cover several hundred yards in a few minutes.

The only time you should not wait is when it is raining. It's amazing how fast rain water can wash away that red sticky blood. I'm very careful when bowhunting in the rain to avoid marginal shots where a bad hit might allow the animal to run off 300 yards before bedding down. If a hunter waits a half hour and then takes up a light bloodtrail, the rainwater may have washed the blood into the ground.

Following The Bloodtrail

An elk does not leave as big a bloodtrail as you would expect from an animal of that size. In fact, an elk's bloodtrail is not much heavier than a deer's. Don't take a light bloodtrail as an indication that the hit was not mortal. Most of the massive bleeding is taking place inside the elk where it will do the most damage.

When you are ready to begin bloodtrailing, go to the spot where the elk was standing when it was hit and search carefully for the first few spots of blood. A bowhunter should pay special attention along the first few yards of the trail to locate the broken arrow shaft. This broken shaft will not only tell how far the arrow had penetrated before it snapped off, but it will also indicate where the hit was made by the color of the blood on it. Bright red, frothy blood indicates a lung shot, rich red blood indicates a liver hit, and dark red blood with food particles in it indicate a paunch hit.

Mark The Bloodtrail

Always mark the bloodtrail as you proceed. Again, I use orange ribbon. If I lose the bloodtrail in heavy brush, I can backtrack to the last spot of blood and begin searching again. Don't become impatient during this bloodtrailing chore and charge ahead to hopefully stumble upon the elk. The best route to your trophy is the one marked by red spots of blood, and as long as you have that bloodtrail, you have a direct route to your elk.

My friend Walt Morkert related an instance to me that points out very well the importance of patience when bloodtrailing. Walt took a safe 30-yard shot at a six-point bull, but the animal turned just after Walt had released the arrow, and the shaft hit the elk in such a way that only one lung was struck. After the elk had crashed off, Walt waited a half hour and then took up the bloodtrail. He was encouraged at first by the heavy trail of blood spots and splashes, but after 100 yards, the copious blood trail had dwindled to a tiny drop every 10 feet. To make matters worse, the bull had fled into a very brushy sidehill where visibility was only about 15 yards.

Walt spent four tedious hours following, losing, backtracking, and refinding the bloodtrail. In all that time, he'd only gone 400 yards. He spent a lot of time on his hands and knees looking for those tiny precious dots of blood lying camouflaged on frost-burnt leaves. Walt's persistence paid off because he found the bull a short time later, and I rough measured it at 280 Pope and Young points.

Field Dressing

The old-timers like to say that the fun is over when the elk hits the ground, and any hunter who has tackled the field dressing chore on an elk would readily agree. A downed bull elk is an awesome sight to behold and an even more awesome chore to field dress. An 800 pound elk carcass lying in a twisted heap on a steep mountainside is a challenge for even the most experienced elk hunter. For the beginner, it can be an exhausting and frustrating experience if he gets intimidated by the size of his task and tries to rush it.

Two Methods Of Field Dressing

There are two methods of field dressing an elk. If horses are available to pack out the elk in quarters, the animal must have its entrails and blood removed and the hide skinned off it. The head and hooves are then removed, and the carcass is split down the backbone with a hatchet and cut in half to create quarters for pack horses. A pack horse can carry half an elk.

The other method is boning. This method is used by hunters who must

Try to locate the broken arrow shaft because it will tell you a lot about how deep the arrow went in and what type of hit you made.

An elk does not leave a large bloodtrail. Often, an elk's bloodtrail will not be any larger than that of a deer.

This bowhunter can pack an elk quarter plus the heavy antlers because he removed the unusable and heavy leg bones.

Meat sacks keep meat free from dirt and contamination by insects.

pack out the game on their backs, and they don't want to pack out even one unnecessary pound over miles of steep, rugged terrain. It is foolish to attempt to backpack out elk quarters. Half the weight of an elk carcass is useless bone, and removing it from the meat will reduce a 150 pound elk quarter to about 80 pounds of meat.

The boning process is simple. The animal does not even need to be gutted if the heart or liver is not taken. First, remove the hide carefully to avoid getting too much dirt on the meat. The largest densities of meat are in the rear hams and front shoulders. You can easily free the leg bone from each ham by cutting along the bone on the inside of the ham. Next come the front legs, which are 60% bone. Use a sharp knife to pare away all the flesh from the shoulder blades and legs.

The last large sections of meat are the fillets which are located on either side of the backbone. The fillets are easily removed by slipping a knife along both sides of them the length of the backbone. Once you have all the large sections of meat removed, go back and slice away all small portions of the hams, shoulders and fillets that you might have missed the first time. Elk meat is too tasty to leave behind, besides being illegal, and the small meat chunks can be ground into burger.

Meat Sacks are Vital

Heavy duty meat sacks are vital when boning out an elk carcass. As you carve each piece of boned meat from the carcass, place it in these sturdy nylon bags. They not only keep the meat free from dirt, but they also make the backpacking chore much easier. When a sack has about 70 pounds of meat in it, tie the end closed and hang it in the shade to cool off.

Two Knives Are Needed

Two knives are necessary to field dress and bone out an elk. Elk hair is coarse and hollow, and it tends to dull a knife blade. That razor sharp knife that you began the field dressing chore with will probably have to be put aside before long and another sharp knife used. Sometimes even that one will be dull before the job is complete. For that reason, I always carry a sharpening steel.

Game Saw And Rope

A game saw is needed for the field dressing chore. Besides quickly severing bone, the saw is needed to cut out a wedge shaped section of skull so that the antlers can be removed without packing out the extra weight of the head. Rope is used to tie up game sacks, but its most important use is to hold the elk securely on its back on steep ground with legs spread out so that the carcass can be field dressed or boned. This is done by tying the legs off to nearby trees.

Field Dressing Kit

I carry a large fanny pack with a big pocket on top and a small one on the bottom. My emergency kit (see Chapter 11) goes in the top pocket, and the field dressing kit goes in the bottom. The total weight of this pack is about six pounds, and the field dressing kit weighs three pounds. My field dressing kit contains:
    4 large nylon game bags
    2 heavy duty knives
    1 game saw
    1 sharpening steel
    30 ft. light rope
    1 small pulley for hoisting bagged meat

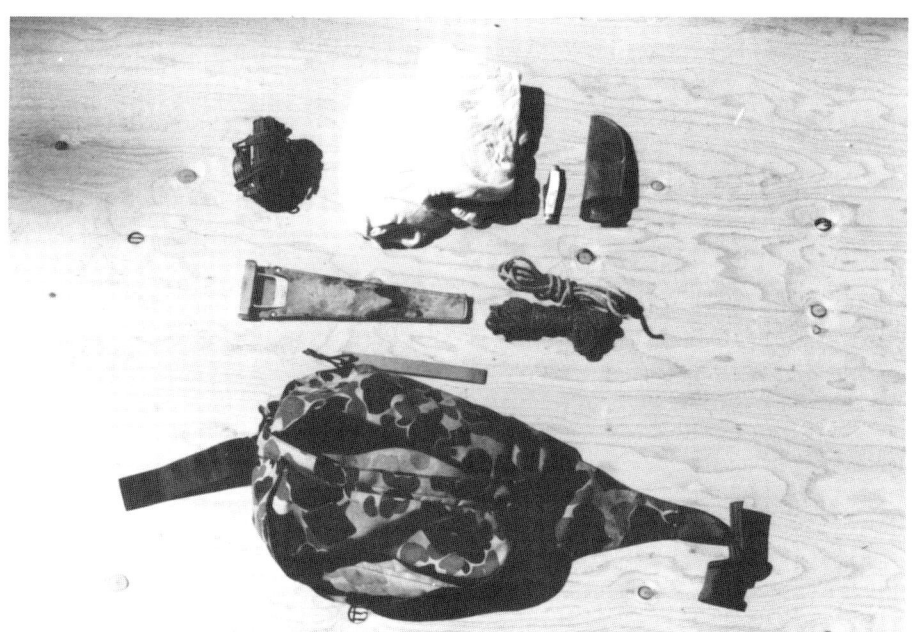
A field dressing kit should contain everything needed to quickly and efficiently field dress an elk.

Packing Out An Elk

Every elk that I have killed with both gun and bow has been packed out on my back, and it hasn't been fun once. It is a backbreaking chore that makes you reassess your preoccupation with the sport of elk hunting. It's bad enough to struggle under all that weight, but when you add steep ground, blowdowns and heavy brush it's enough to make the strongest man's knees wobble.

Unfortunately, it can get much worse. Take all the above and then add the fact that you must pack the meat uphill out of some hell-hole for a couple of miles, and you have the makings for a real ordeal. My friend Walt Morkert helped me pack out an elk from one such hole, and when Walt had finally reached the pickup, he fell to the ground exhausted and gasping for breath. I felt a bit guilty about Walt's condition. It seems that I forgot to mention that it was an uphill pack. I might even have innocently erred and told him that it was a short downhill pack.

After all the arguing and bickering about what I'd told him had died down, I said, "Well Walt, when you get an elk, I'll help you pack it out."

Walt thought for a moment and said, "No, there's only one way for you to make this up to me. If I shoot an elk, I'll draw you a map, and if you pack it out all by yourself, then we'll be even. But at least I'll have enough sense to stay out of a hell-hole!"

The fun quickly departs when the packing begins. My friend Tom Troxel somehow manages a grin during a long hike.

A Good Pack Frame Is Essential

A sturdy, comfortable packframe is worth its weight in gold when packing out an elk. Don't get me wrong. A good packframe will not make a pleasant experience out of it, but at least it won't add to the misery. On the other hand, a cheap, ill-fitted packframe can make the merely unpleasant packing chore more like torture.

Check out a packframe before you buy it. Make sure it has sturdy and well padded shoulded straps, and strong tube aluminum construction. Also, make sure that it has a waist belt to take some of the pressure off your shoulders.

Chapter 10

HOW TO LOCATE RUTTING BULLS

Two things impress the average visiting elk hunter to the Rocky Mountains. The first thing is the immense size of the land, and the second is how difficult it is to locate elk. Sure, there are many thousands of elk in the western mountains, but they are scattered throughout backcountry hideaways. To be successful, a prospective elk hunter must find a specific area to hunt in this vast expanse of rugged mountains, and when he gets there he must know how to locate rutting bulls.

Long Distance Scouting

The solution to this dilemma is scouting, both before and during the hunt. Obviously, a sportsman who lives thousands of miles from the Rockies cannot spend his weekends taking midnight jet flights to Denver airport and then hiking the hills in search of elk. He must use other means of narrowing down the millions of acres of western elk country to a few square miles of land where he will hunt.

The telephone is a sportsman's greatest asset while making a preliminary investigation into promising elk hunting areas. The miracle of electronics allows a fellow from Maryland to dial the phone number of source in the heart of the Rockies for valuable elk hunting information. However, you first need some general idea of an area that is known to produce elk. Appendix A in the back of this book tells which states provide the best elk hunting, and Appendix B explains where the proven elk producing areas are located in every major western elk hunting state. With this information in hand, you are ready to start narrowing down a general area.

The First Scouting Phone Call

The first phone call should go to that state's wildlife agency. Request hunting maps, season dates, and regulations be sent to you. Next, ask to speak to a wildlife biologist. These men are very dedicated and helpful to the sportsman in search of good elk hunting. Get a second opinion on your hunting area. Ask the biologist if it is a good elk producer. Ask if it is rugged, steep country. Find out what the harvest statistics are for that area, such as hunter success rate, total elk harvest, hunting pressure, etc.

After you are through picking his brain, ask if there is a state regional wildlife office near your hunting area. Most states have a statewide office, plus several regionally located offices. The closer you can get to your hunting area, the more specific information you will receive.

Locate A Specific Area To Hunt

The most important piece of information that you should get from a state's regional wildlife office is a more specific area to hunt. For instance, the Gallatin Canyon in Montana is noted in Appendix B as a good elk producer. But that's not enough information to base a hunting trip on. The Gallatin Canyon runs for almost 80 miles! You must find a much more specific location inside this proven elk producing area. A wildlife biologist in this case would surely mention that the Gallatin Canyon area just outside Yellowstone National Park always has elk moving back and forth across the park borders. Aha! You have just narrowed an 80 mile long hunting area down to about five miles. But don't quit there. Try to get the name of a specific side drainage, mile marker, or mountainside where your actual hunting will be done.

Other Sources Of Information

Eventually, you will have gleaned all the information possible from the regional wildlife biologist. Continue on to other sources such as local taxidermists, sporting goods stores, fraternity club members, or friends-of-friends. I know one man who located an excellent hunting area by contacting a fellow Elks Club member in a town near where he wanted to hunt.

The very best source of information for your hunting area will come from other sportsmen who have been there. Let me give you an example. I was bowhunting a wild, backcountry area in northcentral Idaho a few years ago when I met a man from Kentucky who had just killed a dandy five-point bull elk. I was amazed that a nonresident had found this secluded elk paradise, and I asked how he'd accomplished such a feat.

The Kentuckian told me that when he decided to make a western bowhunt for elk, he began asking around his local archery club for infor-

The immense size of the western Rocky Mountains makes locating rutting bulls difficult. (Rich LaRocco Photo)

mation about where to hunt. He received only one positive reply. A friend of his told him that his uncle knew a guy who had hunted in Idaho and had killed an elk. The Kentuckian told me that it took two weeks of digging just to find the guy's address.

The guy told the Kentuckian that the area where he'd hunted was full of elk. The guy had killed his bull with a rifle after the rut had ended, but he said that there were elk rubs all over the place, and he was sure it would be a good place to hunt rutting bulls. Actually, it sounded too good to be true, but when the Kentuckian checked the area out by phone with a wildlife biologist, the story held true. It was a good area to hunt. The Kentuckian hunted in the exact side drainage where the friend-of-a-friend had hunted, and that is where he was the day I met him.

Scouting During The Hunt

When you look at a map of the Rocky Mountains, a five mile square area is smaller than a fly speck. In reality, a five mile square area of rugged Rocky Mountains is a whole lot of country to find an elk in. Consequently, a hunter will have to begin scouting his area as soon as he arrives to locate bugling bulls.

Elk do not live everywhere in the Rocky Mountains. They only live in

The best source of information will come from other hunters who have made western elk hunting trips.

prime habitat, and there are places in known elk producing areas which are not prime elk habitat. The danger here is that a hunter who doesn't know any better might spend his entire trip hunting in an area where there are very few elk, even though the main drainage is an excellent place for elk hunting. This is one of the main reasons why some nonresident hunters fail.

I remember stopping at a camp in Idaho a few years back where three dejected bowhunters were huddled around a fire. I'd just had a terrific hunt about seven miles from their camp in which I'd come very close to killing a bugling bull elk.

The men told me that they were from Georgia, and they had been hunting hard for five days without seeing an elk. As I listened further, it became apparent that they had picked an excellent drainage to hunt elk, but they had no idea where to look for them. Their daily hunting routine was to slowly spread out from camp (located next to a major logging road!) and still-hunt like they did for whitetails back home. They probably never got more than a half mile away from camp all day. You can imagine their excitement that evening when I took them up to the high country where they heard their first elk bugle.

Scouting Comes First

Scouting as soon as you arrive in your hunting area is of critical impor-

This elk wallow is a good place to find rutting bull elk.

Rich LaRocco likes to hunt backcountry because he says the bulls are less wary about confronting a bugling bowhunter. (Rich LaRocco Photo)

tance. Don't get too anxious and rush out aimlessly hunting for a bull elk. First, you have to find one. Spend the first evening after your arrival driving high ridgetop roads and looking over the country. Topographical maps are invaluable for locating prime elk habitat. You can't hike into every secluded drainage looking for prime elk habitat, but with a topo map you can quickly check for prime elk areas near mountain lakes and subalpine terrain.

Scouting for rutting bulls is made easier because the animals are vocal. In the thin high country air, a bull's bugle can often be heard a mile or more away. However, you still must concentrate your scouting trips in areas of prime elk habitat to be successful

Scout In The Backcountry For Elk

Elk are semi-wilderness dwellers. They like the seclusion of isolated backcountry areas far from civilization. Most elk in the Rockies will be found at higher elevations in subalpine terrain. Typical subalpine terrain will have small meadows or openings broken up by patches of timber. The elk like the cool environment of the high country, and they find excellent feed in the lush meadows. Security and shelter are only a step or two away in the heavy timber nearby. There will always be a few elk living down lower near roads, but the most dense populations of elk will be found in the environment just below timberline. A backcountry lake is an excellent place to look for elk. The lush grasses that grow around the water will keep elk in the area.

Another benefit to backcountry hunting is that the bulls are less wary of bugling. Some spots near roads get so much hunting pressure that the bulls become very wary of any bugle, and it is tough to fool them. Bob Mussey told me that he hiked into one small draw during the peak of the rut in Colorado, and there were 12 other bowhunters bugling in that area. Bob said that the bulls may have been crazy with rut, but they weren't stupid!

My friend Rich LaRocco always hunts in remote backcountry areas for this reason. Last fall, Rich packed 22 miles into the Salmon River Wilderness area and killed a huge bull with his bow that scored 340 Pope & Young points. Also, an outfitter friend told me that he has hunted in some places in the Rockies which had good elk populations. However, there were so many bowhunters all bugling at the same time that the bulls actually did very little bugling. They did their rutting silently or at night.

Get High Up To Hear The Bulls

When I scout for rutting bulls, I hike along a high ridge and listen for vocal bulls. I bugle down over both sides of the main ridge, and I'll also hike down finger ridges which branch off the main ridge. The small basins created where these finger ridges meet the main ridge are areas where elk tend to congregate.

A scouting trip is not a casual jaunt of a half mile or so. The object is to locate as many bugling bull elk as possible and then spend the rest of your trip hunting them. My hunting partner Jim Monzie often takes scouting trips of 10 miles or more along a main ridge system. By the time Jim has moved through an area, he has a good idea where all the rutting bulls are

Hike along a high ridge when you scout for elk. That way you will hear any bugling bulls in the surrounding mountains.

located, and he then plans a hunt for the bulls that show the most promise.

Look For Information Sources

Use every source of information to help you find elk. My friend Kelly Johnston told me that one time he was hunting in an area of western Montana that he was unfamiliar with, and he was having problems finding game. His camp was located next to a major logging road, and log truck drivers often stopped to rest in the area. Kelly began chatting with the loggers and asked them if they'd seen any elk in the area. The truck drivers told him of an area where they'd been seeing bulls every morning from the road. Other sources of information might be campers, berry pickers, Forest Service personnel, or hikers. Whoever it is, if they have spent much time in your area, they have probably seen something that would be a valuable aid toward finding elk.

Chapter 11

ELK ARCHERY EQUIPMENT

An elk bowhunter will be faced with several hunting conditions in the West unlike anything he has experienced before. The guy who has spent his bowhunting career sneaking after deer will realize the first time he sees a mighty bull elk that his favorite whitetail bow is too light. There is also an occasional need for longer shots in some western elk country. In addition, shooting conditions for a visiting bowhunter in the steep terrain of the Rockies is both a challenge and a problem.

These special western elk hunting conditions require special archery equipment to deal with the large size of a bull elk and the longer shots often taken in the West. The immediate need of a prospective elk archery hunter is a heavier bow to assure adequate penetration on an elk. The heavier weight bow will also provide flatter trajectory for long range shooting and improved accuracy.

Proper Bow Weight

The problem that many prospective elk bowhunters experience long before their hunt takes place is that they are accustomed to hunting deer, and they experience a great deal of confusion about the correct weight bow to use for elk hunting. They realize that an elk is larger than a whitetail deer, but they wonder how much larger in terms of special equipment needs. If their favorite compound deer hunting bow set at 45 pounds zips arrows through deer back home, can they expect the same performance on elk if they crank up the limbs a few pounds? Or will they need a much heavier bow that threatens to tear out their arm sockets at full draw?

Being a transplanted Pennsylvanian, I understand the confusion that a visiting elk archer might experience. Before my move to Idaho back in 1970, I'd killed a dozen deer in Pennsylvania using a 45 pound recurve. In anticipation of elk hunting in the West, I purchased a 50 pound pull recurve bow.

My initiation to elk hunting in the Rockies was a shock. Besides the difficulty I encountered getting used to the steep, rugged Idaho forests, I was also astounded by the sheer physical makeup of a mature bull elk. They were huge! I realized that an elk was larger than a deer, but my first encounter with a rutting bull elk left me not only with a thrilling, nerve shattering experience, but it also left me in awe of the massive, big boned physique of an elk.

I was fortunate to meet three local bowhunters shortly after I arrived in Idaho, and they invited me to accompany them into some prime backcounty where the elk were rutting. I was still awed and a little intimidated by the vast Idaho forests, and I had very little idea of how to hunt elk with bow and arrow. The local guys would enthusiastically dive into the dense woods at first light and not return until dark, but I hunted closer to the roads where I wouldn't get lost.

One morning I was hunting along the banks of a stream next to a steep mountainside (Do they make them any other way in Idaho?). I was surprised to hear an elk bugle about 400 yards above me. I'd never heard an elk bugle before, but it sounded pretty phony to me. I guessed that it was one of my hunting partners playing a joke on me.

One of the guys had given me a homemade elk bugle made from a 12 inch length of plastic pipe. It was a crude looking thing hastily hacked into shape with a pocket knife. Even worse, it sounded like a kid's flute. I didn't have much faith in this notion of being able to call in a bull elk with a flute-like whistle like you were the Pied Piper. I decided to give it a try anyway, if for no other reason than to humor my devilish hunting partner.

I blew on the bugle and there was an immediate reply. I heard a furious pounding of hoofbeats and the ever increasing sound of brush and limbs crashing. Either King Kong was coming down that mountainside, or it was a bull elk, because a human couldn't have made that much racket. I realized with a shock that I was actually going to encounter the quarry that I was after. The problem was that I wasn't too sure I wanted to!

I didn't have any more time to debate the matter in my mind. Before I was fully prepared for it, a rut crazed bull elk was less than 20 yards away raking his antlers on a clump of brush. I crouched trembling behind a small tree, wondering if I should slip away before the enraged elk found me. I could clearly see the bull through the alders, and I was awed by his immense physical presence. This was not a large deer like I'd expected. This was big, big game.

The bull's large hooves actually sank into the damp forest floor. His massive shoulders and powerful neck lurched forward, and his huge antlers pounded the alders and tore them out by their roots. The other

The urban deer hunter will need special archery equipment to successfully hunt bull elk.

An elk is not a large deer. This bull is big, big game.

thing that impressed me were his bones. That massive shoulder blade looked as formidable as a knight's shield. A sudden shift in the wind brought immediate silence to the forest, and a moment later I was further amazed to see how quickly such a large animal could slip away into the depths of the forest.

That first elk encounter probably caused an overreaction on my part because I went right out and purchased a 70 pound pull recurve bow, and I killed my first three elk with it before I had to admit that it was too much bow for me. I dropped down in weight and purchased one of those newfangled compound bows made by some guy named Jennings.

Over the years, I've pondered the question of the proper bow weight to use on elk, and I must admit that I have wavered back and forth several times between light and heavy bows. Each time that I was on the verge of making a final decision on the matter, some bowhunter would relate his personal experiences that forced me to modify my opinion. However, that nagging question still arises, and I'm asked it at least a dozen times each year. What's the proper bow weight to use on elk?

It's certainly not with the lighter weight bows. There have been a few elk killed with bows in the 45 pound pull range, but everything must be perfect to accomplish it. The arrow must strike a stationary elk between the ribs to gain the necessary penetration. Even the movement of a walking elk is enough to impede penetration from a light bow. Consequently, bows in this range are considered too light for elk.

It is tempting to suggest a minimum bow weight for hunting elk and leave it at that. However, there are several variables such as bow design and efficiency, and broadhead choice, that make it difficult to come up with a single poundage figure.

The modern compound bow is a good example. Late model compounds with cam wheels and overdraw zip out arrows much faster than the same weight recurve or long bow. Consequently, a hunter with a 55 pound pull recurve bow may actually be shooting a slower bow than the guy who uses a 50 pound pull cam bow with overdraw.

More important than actual bow weight is the energy necessary for proper penetration on an elk. An adequate elk hunting bow should deliver a minimum of 50 foot-pounds of energy when it strikes the chest of an elk. But even that figure carries with it a few variables such as broadhead design and shot selection. Also, a bowhunter must be aware that a bow which delivers minimum energy at 15 yards will have dropped off considerably at 40 yards.

Using 50 foot-pounds of energy as a guide, the minimum compound bow weight that should be used on elk should be in the 55 pound pull range. A recurve or long bow should be around 60 pounds. That's the minimum, and it's a figure put forward to open the door to elk hunting for folks with physical limitations who might otherwise reluctantly pass up this tremendous sport. The best bow weight is the heaviest that you can shoot accurately and comfortably. For me it's a 65 pound pull bow, for noted archery expert Dwight Schuh it's a 60 pound compound, and for world traveled bowhunter Chuck Adams it's an 84 pound pull compound.

Heavier Bow Weights Improve Accuracy

The area where I bowhunt elk along the Idaho/Montana border is brushy terrain and shots are usually 30 yards or less, but there are other western areas where the ground cover is sparse and longer shots are required. Consequently, a bowhunter should be prepared to take shots up to 40 yards.

A heavier bow weight will improve the average archer's accuracy because there will be less arrow drop, and the arrow will get there faster, thereby reducing wind drift. An arrow shot from a 50 pound pull bow has a tremendous arch at 40 yards, and the slightest problem with shooting form or release will result in a miss. An arrow shot from a 65 pound pull bow, on the other hand, will have almost two-thirds less arch than the lighter bow, and form and release errors will not have as much impact on the arrow's accuracy. Of course, an archer should not shoot a heavier bow if he has difficulty holding it at full draw.

Broadhead Choice

Most broadheads on the market today are adequate for elk hunting. However, there are noticeable differences in penetration among broadheads, and any bowhunter who is planning to use a minimum bow weight for elk should pay close attention to his choice of broadheads.

The archer who uses a lighter weight bow would be wise to consider using a flat, needle-pointed broadhead such as the Zwickey, Bear, or Magnus type heads. These types of broadheads generally produce greater penetration than the more common bullet shaped broadheads because they cut at the instant of impact and do not force the hide apart in advance of the cutting blades.

That's not to say that the bullet shaped broadheads are inefficient. These types of heads have excellent flight stability and have created a more responsible society of bowhunters because of their factory-sharpened blades. I use Rocky Mountain Razor three-blade broadheads, and I've killed a dozen elk with these heads. But then, I also shoot a heavier bow.

Hunting Arrows

You can kill the biggest elk in the Rockies with one of those inexpensive aluminum arrows sold in discount stores. The arrow is nothing more than the deliverer of the deadly broadhead. However, this is oversimplifying

Proper bow weight is essential to insure proper arrow penetration on a huge bull elk.

There is a noticeable difference in penetration among broadheads.

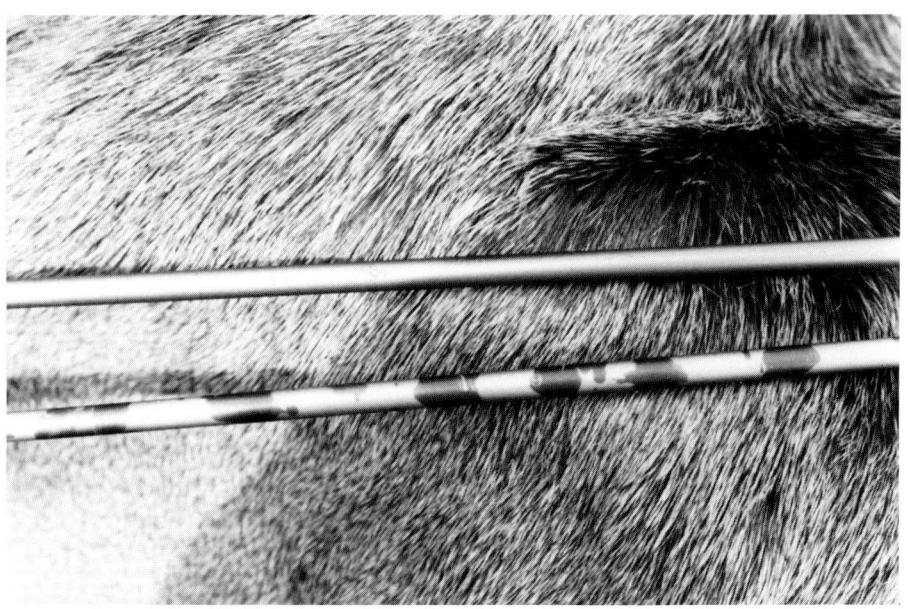

Two favorite shaft colors are burnt orange and camo.

the purpose of one of the important tools of the bowhunter that is often overlooked.

Shaft Selection

Like I said, most inexpensive aluminum arrows are straight enough to insure reasonably accurate flight. The problem is that they bend easily, and when you are fighting through walls of brush and often slipping and falling in the rugged mountains, an inexpensive shaft can quickly take on a permanent bend.

I've taken several nasty falls while pursuing elk in the wild Bitterroot Mountains, and twice my entire body weight came down on the arrows in my quiver. Not once were any bent, and that's the best reason for using higher quality arrow shafts for western elk hunting. My shaft choice? I use XX75 Easton aluminum shafts and I swear by them.

Shaft Colors

A camouflage pattern is the latest coloration craze for hunting arrows, and many bowhunters are attracted to this idea. After all, they reason, if I dress in camo to blend in with the forest, why not do the same thing with my arrows? Sounds like a reasonable deduction, but there are some problems with this type of thinking.

A bowhunter should blend in well with his surroundings, but the half dozen arrows in his bow quiver do not have a great impact on a bowhunter's visibility to game animals. There simply isn't enough surface area to be detected.

Of course, a hunter wants to avoid an obvious stark color such as white arrow shafts. But they don't have to be invisible, either. In fact, an arrow that is too well camouflaged can create more problems than it will solve.

After a shot, it is critical for a bowhunter to find his arrow and inspect it for blood. He might not be able to tell if he hit the animal under low light conditions until he inspects the shaft. In addition, he will be able to tell accurately what kind of hit was made by the type of blood and matter on the shaft. Bright red, frothy blood indicates a lung hit, while dark red blood indicates a hit farther back, etc.

Many wise bowhunters choose burnt orange coloration for their arrow shafts for this reason. The burnt orange arrows blend in well with the forest (animals don't see colors well), but the bowhunter will be able to find the orange shaft even in heavy brush. I've used burnt orange aluminum arrows for many years, and I've been able to locate one of these shafts even when only an inch or two of the shaft was visible above ground.

Camouflage is necessary to conceal the bowhunter from the very prying eyes of an elk.

Archery Practice Tips

A bowhunter after elk often encounters shooting problems due the size of an elk and the rugged shooting conditions typical of elk country. An archer can practice at marked distances at the local shooting range until he becomes frighteningly accurate. However that same archer might miss an open 40 yard shot at a huge bull elk. I've seen this done by guys who couldn't miss while target practicing at camp.

Elk Perspective Is Deceiving

The reason is perspective. An elk is much larger than a mature whitetail deer, but most bowhunters are accustomed to gauging distances from the perspective of the animal's size. Consequently, a big bull elk may step into the open 40 yards away, but to the excited bowhunter he looks like he's only 20 yards away. The result is an arrow that plows into the ground 10 feet in front of the elk because the bowhunter used his 20 yard sight pin to shoot at an elk 40 yards away.

I would suggest that any person planning a western elk hunt should go to a zoo which has elk and practice estimating distances to the elk. This will be an invaluable aid to have had some exposure to the physical presence of an elk. If there are no zoos with elk nearby, go out into the country and gauge shooting distances to horses, which closely approximate the size of a bull elk.

Practice On Steep Terrain

Target ranges are flat. Elk country is not. Oftentimes, a steep uphill or downhill shot must be made. Off balance shots on steep terrain are also common in elk country. An archer should practice these types of shots to become accustomed to shooting where the sight plane between the eye and the target is not comfortably flat. If there is no steep terrain in your area, shoot from the bed of your pickup truck, and do some shooting while balancing on your tiptoes to simulate off-balance shooting. You will be amazed how much your accuracy decreases when you begin practicing this more typical elk country type of shooting.

Camouflage

Camouflage is an important ingredient for the western elk hunter, especially when he moves in to set up a radical challenge. A rut-crazed bull elk who sees a human-like form moving in the area where another bugling bull should have been will quickly disappear. Camouflage also helps a bowhunter avoid detection by cows who might be loitering in the area. I use a one-piece camo jump suit made of light cotton, and I also use camo paint on my hands and face to eliminate glare.

Always identify potential emergency situations. The pristine western backcountry can cause a desperate situation should unforseen problems arise.

Chapter 12

CLOTHING AND EMERGENCY GEAR

Early season elk hunting in the Rocky Mountains occurs during the spectacular Indian summer period when the high country is a serene wilderness paradise with the sun shining. But it is a deceiving tranquility. In a matter of hours, that same idyllic wonderland can quickly turn into unbearable winds, driving rain or sleet, or even snow as early as August in the high country. A hunter who is lulled into carelessness by this pristine beauty in fair weather will pay dearly in terms of discomfort. It might ruin his hunt, or the consequences can even turn tragic.

The western Rocky Mountain states experience definite seasonal weather patterns. The summer season is known for its beautiful sunny weather, with only occasional rain showers to keep the land fresh. This summer weather pattern often runs into September when most archery seasons begin, and bowhunters especially are prone to experience one of the stark realities of the Rocky Mountains in fall — unpredictable weather.

Three years ago the West experienced typical late summer balmy weather, and as Montana's archery season approached that first week in September, most bowhunters were hoping for a storm to cool things off and make the woods more quiet. They got their wish, and more!

The first morning of archery season dawned gloomy, with a light rain falling. Every archer was pleased. An hour later, the drizzle had changed into a drenching downpour driven by 30 miles per hour winds, and most sane bowhunters were driven out of the woods. For the next 22 days it rained, and the forest was awash with water-soaked brush and slippery ground. Any bowhunter who did not have the proper clothing simply could not stand the bone chilling cascade of water every minute of the day.

Of course, the comfortable alternative to fighting this inclement weather was to stay indoors until the storm system passed. That's what most of my bowhunting friends did. They told me that there was no rush, that the elk would still be bugling when the rain stopped. They were wrong. The elk had been in full rut during the stormy weather, and by the time the sun appeared and dried the forest three weeks later, the rut was just about over.

I hunted during that stormy period because I had the proper clothing, and I killed a nice five-point bull. It seems like I'm always wet when I kill a bull elk with bow and arrow. But then, that makes sense because that's when hunting is best.

Bull elk usually rut only in early morning and late evening during fair weather. When the sun appears an hour after dawn, the bulls seek shelter and bed down in heavy cover, and bugling ceases. But when stormy weather moves in, it seems to trigger an added vigor to their rutting instincts, and I've heard elk bugle at all hours during a dismal rainy day when I was the only bowhunter afield.

Clothing Needs

Typical early season weather in the West is brisk and frosty in the morning, but warm in the afternoon. The temperature can climb as high as 80 degrees at midday even in the high country. By late afternoon, however, temperatures will have dropped down to 50 degrees or less. This creates

Autumn in the Rocky Mountains can be deceiving. Balmy weather can turn miserable in a short time.

Light cotton clothing is excellent for early season hunting during fair weather.

A light boot with a Gortex liner is a good choice of footwear.

an obvious problem for the early season hunter. You freeze in the morning and roast in the afternoon, only to freeze again in the evening.

Cotton Clothing For Fair Weather

An elk hunter usually must hike a long distance over rough terrain during the day, and he doesn't want to carry a lot of bulky extra clothing. Most experienced early season elk hunters wear cotton clothing, but they also wear a light down or insulated nylon vest to ward off the early morning and late evening chill. This vest is rolled up into a small bundle and stored in a fanny pack or backpack when not in use.

Wool Clothing Best For Cool Weather

Overcast weather will always be cool, and the temperature will drop from 80 degrees to 50 degrees as soon as the clouds move in. Another thing to remember about storms in the west is that there is no such thing as a warm rain in the high country. The hunter who goes out on an overcast, but potentially stormy, day should leave the cotton clothing behind and wear light wool. I usually wear a light cotton shirt with a light wool shirt-jacket over that, and I wear light wool pants with a tight weave. My friend Dwight Schuh likes to wear wool knickers with knee high wool socks, and he swears by this combination for freedom of movement and warmth.

Footwear

A light boot is a good choice for early season hunting. Even in hot weather, a light boot is advisable to wearing tennis shoes. The rugged western terrain is hard on tender feet, and the added support of a boot will help a hunter unaccustomed to rough country. I would advise any hunter to consider using a light pair of boots with a Gortex liner. This liner will breath away perspiration, but keep feet dry if a sudden storm should hit.

A waterproof boot is valuable even when the weather is not stormy. Usually in September, heavy dew or frost covers the ground vegetation, and a hunter will be soaked half way up his calf. Feet that are wet quickly blister and ruin a promising hunt, but the hunter with a Gortex-lined boot will not even notice the ground moisture.

Headwear

A Gortex lined hat is the best headwear for early season hunting. I use an insultated Jones-style hat for both bowhunting and rifle hunting during the rut. The Gortex liner is critical to keep your head dry when a sudden storm moves in, and the insulation will keep it warm.

Raingear

Raingear is a must for a bowhunter or early season rifle hunter. Early fall storms can drench an entire archery season and last into the early rifle season, and the hunter who is not prepared to hunt comfortably in wet weather might just as well throw away his game tags.

Adequate raingear is one item that nonresident hunters always seem to be lacking. It got so bad when I outfitted that I finally purchased three sets of top quality raingear to loan to clients. I'd tell them to bring rain gear, and they'd show up with a cheap vinyl poncho that cost $6.95! In the cold rain, the brush tore that cheap rain gear to shreds by the end of the first day. By adequate raingear, I mean a complete waterproof outfit of boots, pants, jacket, and hat. With this type of protection, a hunter can hunt hard all day in wet weather and not feel any discomfort from the elements.

The very best raingear is Gortex lined. It not only sheds water, but it also allows perspiration to escape from an overheated body. In my humble opinion, Gortex is a miracle fabric, and I believe that it has greatly improved the potential for hunting success in bad weather. You can outfit yourself from head to toe in Gortex raingear, and that is exactly what I do. I wear gortex lined boots, Gortex pants, Gortex jacket, and Gortex lined hat. Dressed like that, I feel as carefree as a duck in the water.

Besides Gortex raingear, there are also several other major brands of raingear that are adequate. Most of these consist of nylon fabric with a

Good quality raingear is essential for hunting during rainy weather.

vinyl or rubber coating. They are adequate, but they do not allow body heat to escape. After a period of exertion, clothing under the raingear will be soaked in sweat, but the hunter will at least be warm.

Emergency Gear

Anyone planning an elk hunt in the western Rockies should be aware of the potential for emergency situations. A wool shirt on your back and a candy bar in your pocket simply is not enough to insure your safe return if everything does not go according to plan.

The West is big country, and distances between roads are much farther than most hunters are accustomed to. So when an unforseen problem arises, a hunter can't always take a quick hike out of the mountains to safety. When you consider the West's large size and add to that the unpredictable western weather patterns, you have the potential for an emergency situation because an elk hunter will almost always be more than a mile from safety.

There are a host of factors that have led up to tragic situations in the Rocky Mountains in recent years, but none have been more responsible than the weather. A fall day in the West can turn from balmy to a raging blizzard in a matter of hours. Even a rainstorm can mean trouble for the unprepared hunter because a radical drop in temperature always follows a fall storm in the west.

Such unexpected situations that a hunter may encounter while elk hunting do not necessarily become emergencies. Surely, a simple thing like a rain shower in itself is not cause for alarm, but add the fact that the hunter gets lost in his haste to get out of the weather and must spend the night in the woods soaked and exhausted, and you have prime ingredients for a tragedy.

Hypothermia Is The Silent Killer

It is not fair to blame the weather for the disturbing number of tragedies that occur every fall in the western states. Weather doesn't kill men. Neither does hunger or thirst. The West is not that big that a man would starve to death before he found his way out, and water is everywhere in the mountains. The major cause of death among outdoorsmen is hypothermia. It is an invisible, ever-present danger that is more deadly than the meanest grizzly bear.

Hypothermia is nothing more than the lowering of the body's temperature from the normal of 98.6 degrees. It doesn't take a sudden vicious blizzard with below zero temperatures to bring on hypothermia, either. A few years ago, a Montana hiker died of hypothermia while on a summer hike with several companions. A promising sunny morning had degenerated into a cool, drizzly afternoon, and the hiker had not taken

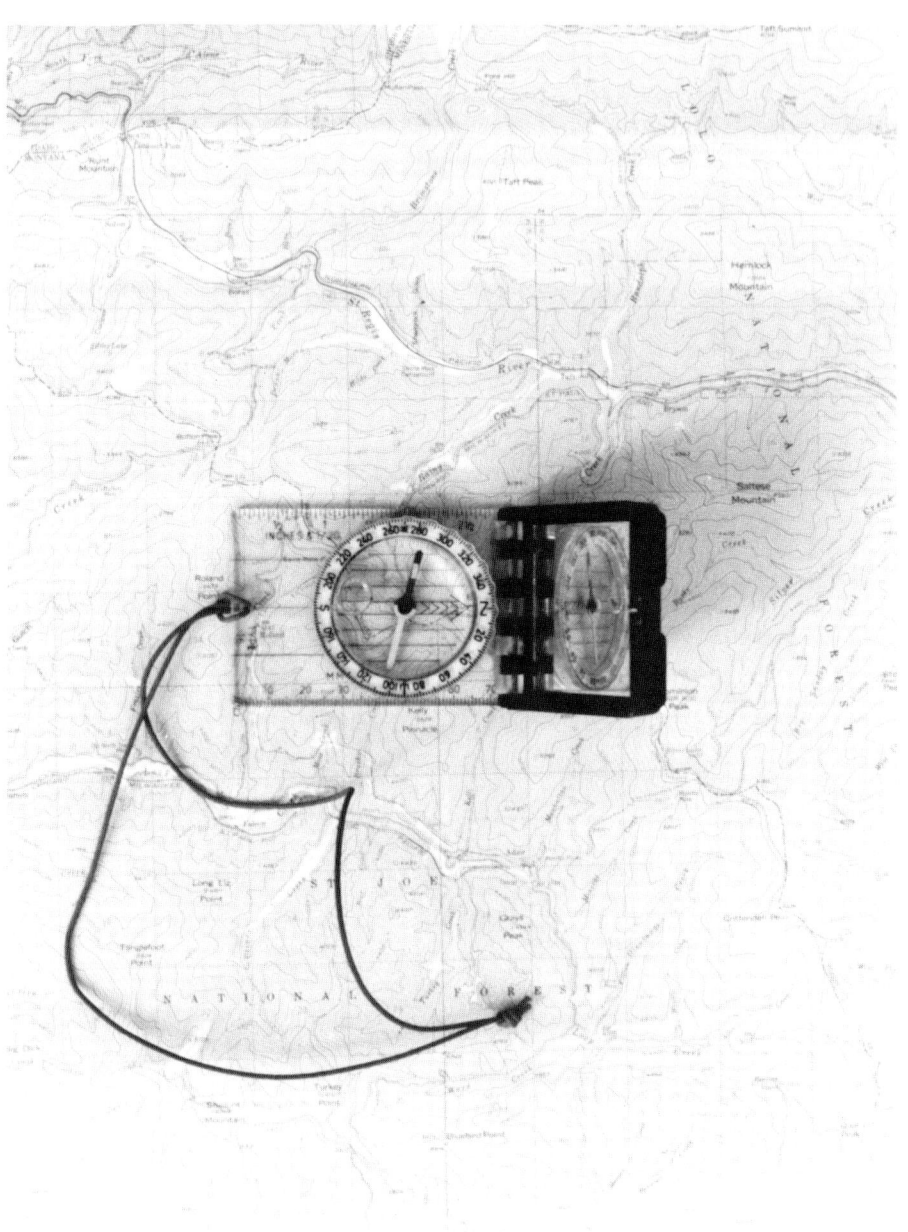

One of the most vital pieces of emergency gear a hunter can carry is a compass. Learn how to use this simple instrument and always be aware of which direction leads to safety.

precautions to keep in his body heat. The result was a man who appeared fine one hour, sluggish the next, and dead an hour later. The bewildering statistic about this entire tragic affair was the fact that the temperature had only dropped to the 50 degree level, yet a man died.

Identify Potential Emergencies

Always assess a western hunt for the potential for emergency situations. Most outdoor tragedies could have been avoided if those victims had just spent a few mimutes thinking out the potential hazards of an upcoming hunt and then took a few precautions.

Look for the obvious areas of concern, identify them, and then take the necessary precautions. For instance, will camp be a long distance from your hunting area? Will the hunt be in the type of rugged terrain where it might be easy to get lost? Is unsettled weather forecast for the time period of the hunt?

Taking Emergency Precautions

Once you have identified the potential problem areas for your upcoming hunt, plan to take the necessary precautions to deal with each particular stituation. Obviously, these precautions will come in the form of an

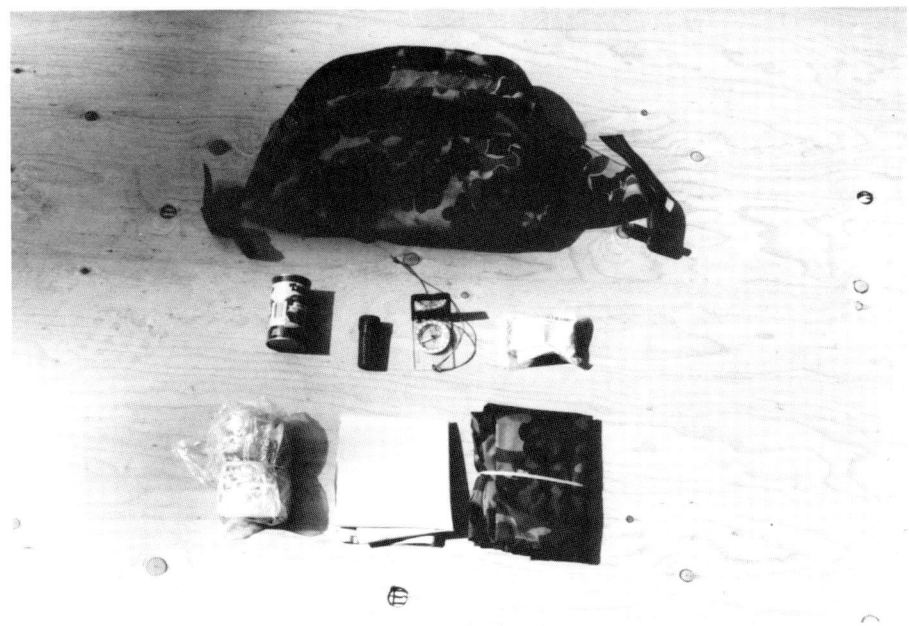

My emergency kit fits in my fanny pack and contains everything I would need to survive an emergency situation.

emergency kit which will contain the necessary equipment to deal with any emergency situation encountered. It is a sad, but true, fact that men's lives could have been saved if they had only thought to take along some waterproof matches or a compass.

Bowhunters especially balk at the idea of carrying along a bulky pack which might restrict their flexibility and shooting form. I carry a large fanny pack with me at all times when elk hunting, and it contains everything I need to field dress an elk or survive an emergency situation. It rests behind me on my hips, and I don't even think about it being there while I'm hunting. Rifle hunters can also carry a fanny pack but most use a small backpack.

Emergency Kit

My emergency kit contains everything that I will need to sustain my life if I'm lost or injured and unable to get to safety. (Weight 3 pounds.) The kit contains:

1 space blanket
1-pound high energy food
1 rollup poncho
1 small can juice
1 pack waterproof matches
1 small flashlight
1 map of area
1 compass
1-6x8 sheet of orange plastic. (For an emergency shelter and visual sighting.)

Chapter 13

PHYSICAL CONDITIONING

Physical conditioning is a vital ingredient for a successful western elk hunt. I'll even take it a step further than that. An elk hunter's chances for success are directly proportional to his physical conditioning. If he is in good shape, his chances of bringing home a trophy are good. If he's in poor shape, his chances are poor. Yet every year many sportsmen make their dream hunt out West for the mighty bull elk in such a poor state of physical condition that their hunt seems doomed from the start.

I believe that outdoor writers such as myself are partly responsible for the general poor condition of the average elk hunter. We relate thrilling western hunts during which elk are all around us, and readers who don't know any better get the mistaken impression that there is an elk behind every tree in the West. We also fail to relay vital bits of information leading up to that special moment when the trophy is sighted. We forget to tell the reader about the exhausting two hour hike uphill in the dark to get to that backcountry elk paradise. Maybe if we could better relate the feelings of burning lungs, gasping breath, low oxygen headaches, fatigue-numbed limbs, we might better make the hunter understand the price that must be paid for that magnificent trophy bull.

When I outfitted, I was continually amazed by clients who had saved for years to make that dream hunt out West for bull elk. I could feel the great buildup of excitement for their upcoming hunt from their letters and phone calls. They made it perfectly clear that they were willing to do anything physically possible to get their trophy. Workout? Oh sure! They had a routine that would put a marathon runner to shame. Yet when they came out West for their dream hunt, they were soft, and they lost elk because of it.

Time and again during the hunt, I'd coax a client up a small hill. Just 50 yards more and the client would have clear shooting at a bull elk. But

Could you do this? Physical conditioning is of critical importance to be successful in the rugged western mountains.

when I looked into the guy's eyes, I could see that the only thing that mattered to him was the ache in his legs, and the burning in his lungs. He wanted the hurt to go away, and at that moment it was more important than killing a bull elk.

There were several reasons why I got out of outfitting, but one of the main reasons was the lack of physical conditioning of my clients. I had a good area to hunt where elk were plentiful, but the country was steep and rough, and few clients came out physically prepared. Consequently, I'd often have disgruntled clients who left camp without their dream trophy, but if those same men had been in a little better shape, they could have gone home with a bull elk.

Not all my clients were like that. A few met the challenge of the Rockies. They paid a price in sweat and pain, but in the end it was worth it because the pain of physical exertion is temporary and usually self-centered. I guided a young man named Jim Kingsley on an elk hunt in western Montana a few years ago, and Jim told me the same old story: "I'll do anything it takes to get an elk." The difference here was that Jim meant it.

One day, I took Jim on a forced march up one canyon, down the other side, and up again after a herd bull. It wasn't much fun for me, and I know

Most nonresidents have difficulty understanding the physical demands that western hunting puts on a sportsman.

Hiking is one of the best ways to get in shape for your hunt. Here, Larry Bennet hikes up a steep hill to get his legs and wind in shape. Larry carries a weighted backpack and hikes in his hunting boots to better simulate actual hunting conditions.

Jim wasn't having much fun either. A couple times when the going got tough while climbing some steep country, he ended up crawling on hands and knees.

There was a reward for Jim's inconvenience and pain. We got into the herd of cows at the perfect time, confronted the bull, and Jim killed him. An hour of inconvenience and some hard breathing paid off for Jim with the trophy of a lifetime and his name permanently noted in the Pope and Young record book. As the saying goes, no pain no gain. And that was exactly Jim's attitude. He now has a great trophy, and a great hunt to remember, but he told me that he also felt a great personal satisfaction that he withstood the great physical challenge of the West and won out.

Getting Into Shape

The radical method of hunting rutting bull elk is an aggressive style of hunting. A hunter is constantly roaming high ridges and listening for bugling elk. When not doing that, he's charging forward to challenge a bull. There is a lot of hiking uphill, downhill, and some forced marches where a hunter must push himself. However, it should be understood that any elk hunting endeavor requires a lot of physical activity because elk prefer backcountry seclusion.

A prospective hunter who wants to get into shape often is confused about what type of exercising to do to tone his body for the upcoming hunt. This is especially troublesome for the guy who lives in an area where there are no mountains to climb. No doubt about it, the best way to get in shape for climbing mountains during the hunt is to do a lot of uphill hiking. However, there are a few alternative exercises that will strengthen the calf and thigh muscles. Jogging, bicycle riding, swimming, and gym workouts all help to tone the body for the hunt.

Hiking

Hiking is the best way to train for your upcoming hunt because that is essentially what elk hunting is all about. Long hikes on flat ground are better than nothing, but the ideal terrain for hiking would be rolling hills where your legs experience both the strain of going uphill, and the shock of coming down. Some hunters in training also hike with a pack on their back to simulate the added weight they will be carrying during the hunt. This weight can be increased daily. My friend Bob Mussey from Wisconsin works up to a 50 pound pack before his elk hunts.

One mistake that sportsmen make when hiking to get in shape is that they ignore the punishment that their feet will take during the hunt. They do a lot of hiking, but in light tennis shoes which are made to cushion the feet. However, the first time during the hunt that a hunter endures a long day hiking over rough terrain, his feet may blister badly, thereby restricting

Jogging is an excellent exercise for improving breathing and circulation for an upcoming hunt.

him to camp for the next two days until his blisters heal. Avoid this problem by hiking in the same boots that you will be using during the hunt.

Jogging

Jogging is an excellent exercise for improving cardiovascular circulation. A jogger routinely feels lightheaded when his heart and lungs cannot supply the oxygen demands of his hard working body. The more a jogger works out, the better his heart and lung function to supply oxygen to his brain and tired legs. This is exactly the problem that a hiker has in the western mountains. He pushes his body, but his heart and lungs can't keep up. Consequently, jogging is of vital importance when working out for an upcoming hunt. Jogging is primarily intended for improving a hunter's wind. While it is also helpful for overall body tone, it does not do enough for the legs and thighs.

Bicycling

I guided a group of hunters one year, and while two of them had problems with the steep terrain, one of the men did quite well. The other two men had jogged and worked out in the gym. The third man jogged too, but he also began riding his bicycle to work. His legs at first ached from the five mile ride every morning and afternoon, but in a short time they became stronger and he pushed them even more. By the time he came out West, his calves and thighs were in excellent condition for hiking.

The pumping motion of bike peddling closely resembles the uphill hiking rythm of a hunter's legs. This is the best exercise for the hunter who does not have any hills or mountains to climb. Don't forget, the object is to push yourself, so you might want to refrain going through all the gears on your 10-speed. Instead, let the bike lug down and use your leg muscles to force the bike forward.

Swimming

Swimming is excellent for overall body tone. In addition, swimming expends more energy than any other exercise. It improves your wind, plus it strengthens your leg and stomach muscles. Most gyms and health clubs have pools. A good workout would be to jog, hit the weight room, and then swim. Body tone and increased physical capacity will surely result from this routine.

Weight Room

Weightlifting is not the best method of getting in shape for hunting. While it does improve overall body tone, lifting weights does not do

Altitude conditioning is important if you plan to hunt at high elevation in the Rockies.

enough for improved lung capacity and leg drive like other exercises. However, there are a few exercises that definitely improve leg strength. The first exercise is squats. You bring a barbell of weights above your head and rest them on your shoulders, and then you do deep knee bends. Thigh and calf muscles quickly fatigue under the strain of the barbells. A gym with a weight machine also has an exercise that strengthens the legs. You lay on your back and push up against any predetermined weight with your legs, and this exercise is especially good for the thighs.

Step Test

The Forest Service has a test to determine the physical condition of firefighters. A person stands in front of a bench and then steps up onto it and then back down. It sounds simple doesn't it? That's what everyone thinks when they first start out, but after a few minutes, leg and thigh muscles begin to ache, and soon they are screaming to quit. Any prospective hunter who does not have a hill to hike up should spend about 15 minutes per day doing the step test.

High Altitude Conditioning

Altitude is a problem that most hunters overlook when conditioning for a western hunt. Here's a typical situation. A guy from New York City is planning a hunt for elk in the Wind River Country of Colorado. The elevation of New York City is 100 feet above sea level, while the good elk country in Colorado is found at about 8,000 feet above sea level. The air is much thinner at that elevation, and the guy who has not improved his lung capacity will feel like he's run into an invisible wall when he starts hiking up one of those seemingly endless Rocky Mountains.

Obviously, there's not much that a man from the lowlands can do to perfectly simulate those high altitude conditions, but there are a few things that he can do to improve his understanding of thin air exertion. Mount Marcy, (elevation 5,344 ft.) in the nearby Adirondack Mountains is only a two hour drive from New York City, and it is the highest peak in New York state.

Mount Marcy is also readily accessible by trail to the top. If the guy from New York City was smart, he'd take a couple of hikes up to that elevation during the summer before his trip to improve both his leg strength and wind. The feeling of light-headedness he gets at the top will help him recognize and be prepared for the limitations that the Colorado high country will put on him.

A bull elk bugling.

Chapter 14

THE CONDITION OF OUR WESTERN ELK HERDS

There is a vast difference between our present day elk herds in the Northern Rockies and what Lewis and Clark found 180 years ago. The famous explorers wintered in the Bitterroot Range of the Rockies along the Idaho/Montana border during their epic journey, and they almost starved to death. There were very few deer in the gloomy virgin forests, and no elk.

Today this same area harbors one of the highest densities of elk in the West, and almost 10,000 animals are harvested annually. This is a wildlife success story that very few folks in times past would have believed, especially Lewis and Clark. What happened between 1808 and 1988 to bring about this explosion of the elk herd?

Elk Were Once Plains Dwellers

It is common knowledge that elk were plains dwellers when Lewis and Clark explored the West. And for good reason. The northern Rocky Mountains were covered with a continuous carpet of virgin forest. Beautiful groves of majestic white pine, red fir, spruce, and cedar trees towered over 100 feet above the forest floor, and their tight woven canopy of limbs created a gloomy environment down on the forest floor.

The ground below was pretty to walk through, but it wasn't much for plant growth. In fact nothing grew down below the virgin forest due to the lack of sunlight. No plant life meant no wildlife. Early day explorers and surveyors throughout the West noted the absence of wildlife, except for black bears which dug insects from rotting tree stumps and logs. In the meantime, the plains were being rapidly settled, and the opportunistic pioneers quickly eliminated the stately elk herds from the great plains.

Virgin forests of huge trees like this white pine carpeted the West a century ago and provided very little prime elk habitat.

Elk Were Scarce In 1900

For almost 100 years, the only elk in the Northern Rockies were found in a few isolated pockets where small meadows afforded meager feed. Suddenly in 1900 a series of cataclysmic events occurred throughout the West that would eventually send the elk population skyrocketing. A series of wildfires had scorched large sections of dense virgin forest in the first few years of the new century, but the famous 1910 fire outdid them all.

Fires Open Up The Forest

This holocaust created a tornado of fire that swept through the Northern Rockies. A huge smoke cloud spread outward and blotted out the sun for weeks throughout the West and Midwest, and when this smokey pall had cleared, early day Forest Service employees discovered to their horror that there was nothing left. In less than 48 hours more than nine billion board feet of timber had gone up in smoke. The huge trees and gloomy forest had disappeared, and only a blackened moonscape remained.

It was a horrifying disaster in terms of lost timber and human lives, but unknown to discouraged federal land managers, there would soon grow forth a new crop every bit as valuable as the lost timber. Foresters decreed that the fire had burned so hot that most of the scorched earth was sterile and would never again grow anything. In three years the barren mountains were covered with lush green grasses and a profusion of brush.

Elk Replaced Timber As A Valuable Crop

There was no reason for humans to venture into these ugly burned over areas, so few folks knew or cared what was going on in the old burns. There was plenty going on. Deer, elk, and bear moved in and flourished in this endless glut of vegetation. Within 10 years, elk could be seen on almost every sidehill by local folks who had never before laid eyes on such an animal.

The Elk Decline

Harvest statistics illustrate well the dramatic increase in the elk herd. In 1900 about 3,000 elk were killed in the West, but by 1920 the harvest had jumped up to 20,000. The elk harvest peaked in the 1960's at about 140,000. Shortly after this peak harvest period, several of the top elk states experienced noticeable dips in the elk harvest in some of their prime hunting districts. By 1970, nagging little problems concerning the western elk herds which had been ignored through the years of prosperity began to have an impact on the elk herds.

The difference between elk hunting today and elk hunting during that peak period 20 years ago illustrates the degree to which elk have declined. Twenty years ago, most western elk hunting seasons opened in September and stayed open until December by which time every hunter who wanted one had killed an elk. You could also shoot either sex back then. Today, elk seasons have been shortened drastically, and some areas now allow only a five day elk season. Also, cow elk harvest has been greatly restricted in an attempt to bolster declining elk herds, and most western states now require a nonresident drawing or quota to control hunting impact.

The Reason For The Decline

The reason for the decline in elk hunting from the golden years for the most part can be traced back to the source that had created the elk explosion. The habitat had changed. Entire burned over mountain ranges which had exploded into lush rolling carpets of prime elk vegetation had slowly matured and outgrown the reach of the wintering elk herds.

It is shocking to look at old photos of this habitat from the 1930's when it was in its prime for elk. Lush grasses, waist-high brush, and young coniferous trees covered naked mountains. Look at the same mountains today, and you would be hard pressed to guess that a devastating fire had ever burned there. The timber has grown up, once again blocking out the vital sunlight, and the valuable winter food supply of vine maple and alder brush has also slowly outgrown the 10 foot reach of an elk feeding on its hind legs. Basically, the mountains are slowly returning to the elkless virgin forests of 1900.

Civilization's Encroachment On Elk

While this was going on, man-made encroachment was also adding to the impact on elk herds. The vast resource potential of the West was being tapped. Mining exploration and construction were booming, logging was going full bore, and ranchers had discovered that the western backcountry was excellent habitat for their cattle. Add to all this the sudden discovery by our nation's sportsmen of the trophy potential of the bull elk, and you have an invasion by a vast army of hopeful sportsmen to the western Rockies which were being exploited by progress and outgrowing their usefulness as prime elk habitat.

This sudden awakening to the decline of the western elk herds sent shock waves through state wildlife agencies and up through the federal Forest Service. Previously, wildlife officials tended to be more concerned with the elk harvest. If decline in the elk herds was to be stopped, intense habitat management was also necessary.

Today's Intense Elk Management

Today, intense elk habitat study and improvement is being practiced by state and federal wildlife officials throughout the West. Overgrown brush fields are being burned so that new browse can grow. Certain forested areas of poor elk habitat are being logged specifically to create wildlife feeding areas in the backcountry. Logging is now carefully planned and monitored to insure minimum impact and ultimately improve the land. In addition, intense elk studies have been made to better understand how logging, mining, grazing, and general human encroachment affect elk. And last, there is a concentrated effort throughout the west to upgrade the trophy potential of the average bull elk.

Logging Gets A Bad Rap

Logging has taken the brunt of the criticism from alarmed sportsmen and conservation groups concerning elk habitat. The standard logging practice of creating large clearcut areas has especially come under fire in recent years, and frustrated conservationists have even leveled the charge

A series of devastating forest fires ravaged the West beginning in 1900. Virgin timber was lost, but elk moved into areas where profuse plant growth appeared a year later.

of conspiracy between the Forest Service and loggers. No doubt about it, logging has had an impact on elk populations in the West. Some of the impact has been bad, but some of it has been beneficial, and some of the controversial logging that has received much of the criticism simply had to be done.

The Clearcut

A forest of trees is a renewable resource. It grows to maturity, declines, and then dies much like a field of corn in Iowa. No one screams rape at the Iowa farmer who harvests his land because folks have seen with their own eyes the capacity of that Iowa field to regenerate another crop. With trees, it's the same thing, but instead of a new crop every year, it's a new crop every 60 years. Folks on vacation visiting the western forests are aghast at the ugly spectacle of a clearcut forest. Where there was once a beautiful forest, now they see only treeless desolation, with nothing growing in it but grass and scrub brush.

However, if they would take the time to walk through a logged over area, they would immediately notice that it had been burned so that most of the logging slash and small stunted trees were removed. Also, five

My home in western Montana had no elk until men with forethought transplanted several animals in 1913. Today, this is one of the best elk hunting areas in the West.

years after a clearcut has been carved out of the forest, a staggered profusion of young coniferous trees can be seen popping up above the low brush, the result of an aggressive Forest Service tree planting program. But most importantly, a visitor hiking through a clearcut will notice a lot of elk tracks and droppings. That clearcut has created the exact condition of profuse grass and brush growth that had occurred after the 1910 fire, only on a smaller scale. In 20 years after the brush has outgrown the reach of the elk, the trees will have grown up enough to begin choking out the overgrown brush, and a mature forest will eventually result.

Roads Create The Greatest Impact On Elk

The greatest adverse impact on elk that logging creates is access roads. Elk are large animals that require the seclusion of semi-wilderness areas. They cannot live in tiny pockets of timber very near civilization like a whitetail deer. Every road that dissects the western forest has an adverse impact on the elk herd. It is proven fact that elk avoid well-roaded areas where human activity is high. Recently, the Forest Service has begun closing off logging roads to motorized vehicles immediately after logging has ceased. This practice has greatly improved elk habitat in heavily logged areas. However, it is not popular among sportsmen who don't want to work for their elk.

There are some areas in the west that have been logged too much, with adverse impact on the elk herd. Some of this was the result of self interest by loggers, but much of it was done to get some benefit from a dying forest. A good example of this is the Simmons Creek drainage in the St. Joe National Forest of northern Idaho. The first time I drove up the Simmons Creek road, I was shocked by the total devastation to the land. Thousands of acres of clearcut stretched for miles. I concluded that this was clearly an example of mad-dog loggers gone wild. However, the facts in this situation proved otherwise.

Back in 1960, Simmons Creek was a virgin forest of valuable white pine. A small amount of logging was done, but care was taken to insure a large buffer of timber between openings. However, a disease called "blister rust" swept through northern Idaho and devastated the white pine forests. Simmons Creek was especially hard hit. Foresters told me that in a matter of months, the green tree tops of the white pine forest had begun to turn red as the needles died.

In a few years, this fabulously rich white pine forest would have been reduced to a snag patch. A hurry-up effort was made to get most of the white pine timber logged before it went bad, and the result was a continuous string of clearcuts. Farther down along the St. Joe River, the white pine was not saved, and today it is an ugly snag patch with a thick mat of scrub cedar growing underneath that chokes out browse and grass, and very little wildlife lives there.

The State Of The Northern Rockies Today

There are new environmental problems popping up every year throughout the West which have an impact on the elk herd. It may be a silver mine in the Cabinet Wilderness area of western Montana, or a new ski resort planned for prime elk habitat in the Colorado Rockies. In Idaho, it may be logging, while in Arizona overgrazing by ranchers may be the problem. The West is growing. Folks like to live there, and the ingenuity of the human mind is continually dreaming up new ventures to sustain a modern standard of living.

There is also a lot of good news about the western elk herds. State and federal agencies have received the support of both nonresidents and western sportsmen to maintain, rebuild, and improve the western elk herds. In some areas where elk were scarce a few years ago, huntable populations now exist due to intense habitat and species management. The nonprofit group, the Rocky Mountain Elk Foundation, has exploded in recent years with the enrollment of thousands of concerned citizens from every state in the union. Critical winter feeding ranges for elk are being purchased by this organization and managed specifically for elk.

Even hunting is now controlled to insure a healthier elk herd. States such as Colorado, which harbor a vast elk herd and impressive harvest

The much maligned clearcut may look unsightly, but provides much of the critical food for today's elk herds in forested areas.

but few mature bulls, have now instituted new regulations banning the harvest of spike bulls in some areas. Only branch antlered bulls are fair game, and already there has been a marked upgrading in the trophy potential of bull elk in these areas. Yes, the West is ever changing. Not always for the best, but not always for the worse, either. The advance of civilization is inevitable, but there will always be a vast federal wilderness and national forest system in the West where any citizen can hunt. It's your land, and it's my land, and no man can ever tell us that we can't hunt there. As long as we have this national federal land treasure, and dedicated men to manage it, we sportsmen will always have a place to go where we can hear the challenging bugle of the bull elk in rut.

Appendix A

STATE BY STATE COMPARISON

This is a state-by-state comparison of the best elk hunting states in the west, beginning with the top state and on down. Use this appendix to decide which western state is the best for your elk hunting trip, and then refer to Appendix B for the best proven elk producing areas in that state.

Colorado

Colorado is the top rated western state for elk hunting, with a vast herd of 155,000 animals, and an annual harvest of about 30,000. In addition, many nonresidents find Colorado's licensing system very attractive because every sportsman who applies for a license gets one. There is no nail biting while you wait to see if your dream hunt must be postponed because you weren't drawn for a tag.

As a result of these attractive figures and features, Colorado is heavily hunted. About 200,000 hunters crowd into the prime elk hunting areas each fall, and hunter success is about 12% — decent, but not great.

The hunter who wants to hunt elk and is not concerned with bringing home a trophy size bull should find Colorado a good elk hunting state. But the guy who has his heart set on a place where his chances of killing a big bull are good might want to explore what other western elk states have to offer. Don't get me wrong, there are some big bulls in Colorado, but they are mostly located in the very rugged backcountry where hunting pressure is light, and most nonresidents will never get to.

However, there is some good news concerning Colorado's status as a trophy bull elk hunting state. A few years ago, the state set new regulations banning the killing of spike bulls in the prime Wind River country of northwestern Colorado. By now, this attempt at upgrading the size of the average bull elk should be paying off, and the potential for killing a branch antlered bull should be much better than the poor reputation that Colorado currently has as a trophy elk state.

Montana

Montana is recognized as the top western state for trophy bull elk hunting, with 52 entries in the Boone & Crockett record book. The Big Sky state has a large, well dispersed elk herd of about 150,000 animals, and hunters kill about 15,000 elk annually.

Huntable populations of elk exist today in many areas where elk were scarce 10 years ago, largely because of intense wildlife management.

The elk herd is so well dispersed that hunting pressure never gets so intense that hunters feel crowded. As a resident of this state, I'm surprised that several very productive areas where I hunt hardly ever see hunters. Elk hunting in these lightly hunted areas is excellent because the potential for finding a trophy size bull is much better, and the bugling is always better when the woods are not full of bugling hunters.

A drawback to elk hunting in Montana has been its first-come, first-served policy of issuing its 17,500 nonresident combination licenses (elk, deer, bear). In the past, there has been a mad rush for these licenses. But recently, this logjam has been eased and any nonresident who is prompt can expect to receive a license. In addition, Montana now allows a special antelope-deer license for nonresidents who don't want to hunt elk, thereby freeing the combination licenses to folks who are primarily after elk.

Idaho

Idaho is in the middle of the pack, with a yearly harvest of about 11,000 elk out of a herd of 106,000 animals. There are 25 Idaho elk entered in the Boone & Crockett record book, and I believe that this state is a "sleeper" for trophy bull elk. I hunt there every year, and I can personally attest to the fact that there are still lots of trophy size bulls roaming within a mile of public highways.

Idaho is often passed over by elk hunters because of its difficult terrain. Typical elk terrain is very steep and rugged, with heavy brush. In fact, the brush continues right up to timberline in some areas, therby limiting visibility and increasing frustration. Consequently, hunters with physical limitations should be careful where they plan their Idaho hunt. There are a few elk areas with moderate terrain, but not many.

Wyoming

Wyoming is another state in the middle of the pack, with an annual elk kill of about 15,000 from a herd of about 75,000 animals. However, Wyoming is well known for its trophy elk hunting, with 42 bulls in the record book, second only to Montana, and it boasts the highest overall hunting success rate of about 30%.

However, Wyoming is burdened by two bewildering laws which greatly hinder its rise to the top for nonresident elk hunters. First, it issues all of its nonresident elk tags on a lottery basis. Consequently, you must keep all your elk hunting plans on hold until you find out if you were drawn for a license. Your chances are 50-50 for being drawn.

The second problem area is the law that requires nonresidents who hunt the wilderness areas where much of the top elk hunting is located, to use a guide. No problem if that's what you'd planned to begin with, but if you've planned a self-guided elk hunt, be careful to center your hunt in a non-wilderness area.

Wyoming is spectacularly beautiful country, with huge, steep mountains and high country meadows. It's also taxing for the hunter with physical limitations, so be careful to pick an area with moderate steepness if you are not able to hike in steep terrain.

Oregon

Oregon ranks second only to Colorado in total elk harvest, with an annual kill of about 20,000 out of a herd of 93,000 animals. But these figures lose much of their luster when you consider that Oregon has only six bulls in the Boone & Crockett record book. In addition, the bull-cow ratio in some heavily hunted areas is very low, about four mature bulls per 100 cows.

The prime elk hunting areas receive intense hunting pressure and the majority of harvested bulls are spikes. Consequently, you would have to consider Oregon to be a good state to hunt elk, but not trophy elk. Unfortunately, things will probably not get much better due to the large population centers along the Oregon coast where most of the elk hunting is located.

Washington

Washington has some decent statistics concerning elk. Hunters kill about 11,000 animals every year from a herd of about 62,000. However, the success ratio is a slim 7%, and there are only two Yellowstone elk in the Boone & Crockett record book. This is due to the limited range of the elk herd, which is confined to pockets of prime habitat where large numbers of hunters often create unbearable hunting pressure.

There are some bright spots for Washington elk hunting. Much of the mountainous elk terrain in Washington is moderate, and there is even some flat ground elk hunting done in the northeast and West Coast areas. Consequently, a hunter with physical limitations could find many suitable elk hunting areas. In addition, the elk hunting in the mountains of Washington is done at moderate elevations of about 3,000 feet, which may be more attractive to the hunter who has problems with thin air.

Arizona

Arizona has about 18,000 elk, and hunters take about 1,900 of them every year. Because of these lower numbers, Arizona is not considered to be a top elk state overall. But in this case, the numbers are a bit deceiving.

Arizona grows big elk! Considering its relatively small elk harvest, there are a whopping 18 bull elk in the Boone & Crockett record book, and the chances of a hunter killing a trophy bull are excellent.

Unfortunately, a hunter must first obtain a license, and competition is tough. In addition, a lot of the elk hunting in Arizona is on private ranches or Indian reservations which charge healthy fees and tightly control the number of permits to insure quality hunting. That's the secret of all the big elk in Arizona, which is not a bad idea.

Any hunter who wants the best chance to take a top elk trophy should consider Arizona. Sure, you might need a little patience when applying for a licence, but remember, Arizona has by far more record book elk than any other state when you consider its total harvest.

Arizona is another state that offers elk hunters with physical limitations some moderate hunting ground. Some of it is high country park-like terrain, but there are also some moderate slopes even up high that are fairly easy to hike over.

New Mexico

New Mexico has an elk herd of about 15,000 with an annual harvest of about 2,000 and an 11% success rate. Competition is fierce for the limited number of elk licenses issued annually, and state officials are determined to slowly bring all public elk hunting up to trophy level. In fact, several huge ranches and Indian reservations now offer limited hunting which provide exceptional trophy potential. Of course, the cost of this private ground hunting is high.

New Mexico elk hunting is mostly at high elevations, but the terrain is not too steep. Consequently, a hunter with physical limitations could do well if he could handle the thin air.

Appendix B

BEST PROVEN ELK AREAS

This is a state-by-state reference to the best proven elk producing areas in each state. Use this appendix to begin your search for a specific elk hunting spot. First contact should be that state's regional wildlife agency.

Arizona

1.) One of the best elk areas in this state is located north and east of Springerville on U.S. 666 in south Apache County and farther south to Alpine.

2.) Another good elk producing area takes in the mountains just north of the Fort Apache Indian Reservation. This also includes the reservation, which allows limited hunting by permit on a fee basis.

3.) In the northern part of the state, elk in good numbers are found just north of the Grand Canyon on the Kaibab Plateau south of Jacob Lake on U.S. 89A.

4.) The Mogollon Rim country which extends north of the Fort Apache Indian Reservation is always good for elk. Best hunting is south of U.S. 66 below Holbrod in Sitgreaves National Forest.

5.) The high country forests immediately east and south of Flagstaff on I-17 in Coconino County are excellent for elk.

Colorado

The northwest and southwest corners of Colorado produce its tremendous elk herds. Herds in the north are more localized, with large elkless areas between them. In the southwest, terrain is more suitable, so the elk are more evenly distributed. The top 10 elk hunting counties are Rio Blanco (unit 12), Routt (unit 14), Gunnison (unit 23), La Plata (unit 24), Archuleta (unit 74), Larimer (unit 76), followed by Mineral, Eagle, Grand, and Hinsdale.

1.) In the southwest part of the state, one of the best elk hunting areas is around the Purgatory Ski Area in unit 74 in the San Juan Mountains. This area is located 25 miles north of Durango on U.S. 550 in La Plata County. Take Forest Service road No. 578 from U.S. 550, which leads to Purgatory.

2.) In the southwest, another good area is found due north of Pagosa Springs on U.S. 160 in Archuleta County all the way to the Continental Divide. Also, the area north and south of Vallecito Reservoir is good for elk.

3.) A vast elk herd inhabits the Flat Top Wilderness Area on the White River Plateau in the White River National Forest. Try Piceance and Yellow creeks south of the White River and southwest of Meeker on U.S. 13-789 in Rio Blanco County.

4.) The entire area around Steamboat Springs on U.S. 40 in Routt County is excellent for elk. This area is located in the Routt National Forest. Specifically, try Elk Creek north of Steamboat Springs, and Trout Creek to the south.

5.) In the southwest, good elk hunting is found in the Uncompahgre Plateau area of the Uncompahgre National Forest. Try the area southwest of Delta and Montrose on U.S. 550 in Montrose County. This is high, rough, and wild country.

Idaho

It does not do justice to this state to name a few drainages and leave the reader with the impression that those are the only good spots for elk. Virtually all of the forested land in central and northern Idaho is good elk country. The exception is the area north of Pend Oreille Lake near the Canadian border, which has a light elk population. Some of the following descriptions may seem vague, but the intent is to show the widespread heavy distribution of elk in those areas. Statistically, the top three elk producing areas are Chamberlain Basin, the Lochsa River, and the Selway River, all in northcentral Idaho.

1.) In the eastcentral part of the state, the vast Selway-Bitterroot Wilderness Area is the top elk producer. The Lochsa, Selway, and Clearwater river drainages are evenly matched for productivity throughout. Two good jumping off points are the towns of Kooskia on state route 13, and Elk City on state route 14. This is rugged, steep backcountry with very limited road access, but lots of elk.

2.) In the central part of the state, the River Of No Return Wilderness Area is one of the top elk hunting areas. This area lies due south of the Selway-Bitterroot Wilderness. Best areas are the Hell's Half Acre area, along with the area around Deep Creek campground. Excellent hunting can also be found down the Selway River drainage and to the north around Beaver Jack and Cayuse mountains.

3.) In the western part of the state, the Hell's Canyon Recreation Area along the Oregon border is excellent for elk. This area takes in the Snake River drainage north of Weiser on U.S. 95 in Washington County.

4.) The entire North Fork Clearwater River drainage north of the town of Pierce on state route 10 in Clearwater County is very good elk hunting. Elk are found virtually everywhere, and good hunting can be found near main access roads. Try Kelly Creek north of the Kelly Creek Ranger Station, and Black Canyon for good elk hunting. This area is in the Clearwater national Forest.

5.) Excellent elk hunting can be found in north Idaho in the entire St. Joe River drainage east of St. Maries on U.S. 95A in Benewah County. In particular, try the upper St. Joe country east of Avery all the way to its headwaters at St. Joe Lake. Every side drainage of the St. Joe has good elk hunting.

6.) Another excellent area for elk hunting in north Idaho lies in the entire North Fork Coeur D'Alene River drainage north of Kingston on I-90 in Kootenai County. In particular, try the area around the McGee Ranger Station and north. This area lies in the Coeur D'Alene National Forest.

Montana

Montana has so many excellent elk hunting areas that you could hunt almost any forested area southwest of Bozeman and west of Butte and not go wrong. Generally, the western forests hold the largest populations of elk, but there are a few isolated mountain ranges in the central part of the state such as the Big Snowy and Bear Paw mountains that are also good elk hunting. Some of the following descriptions may seem a bit generalized, but in certain areas vast tracts of forest are prime elk habitat, and elk hunting is excellent throughout.

1.) In the far western part of the state, the entire Bitterroot Mountain Range along the Idaho line from the Canadian border south to Yellowstone National Park is all excellent elk hunting. I should know, that's my stomping grounds. One really good spot lies west and south of Thompson Falls on U.S. 200 in Sanders County. Another top spot is the Great Burn Roadless Area south of Superior and Alberton in Mineral County. Farther south, the Lolo Pass area on both sides of U.S. 12 southeast of Missoula is excellent elk hunting.

2.) In western Montana, the most productive and famous elk hunting area is the Bob Marshall Wilderness area southeast of Kalispell on U.S. 93 in Flathead County. The area around and south of Spotted Bear Ranger Station in the Flathead National Forest is a good place to center your search for a specific elk hunting spot, but the Bob Marshall is good elk hunting throughout. Horse hunters especially like the Bob Marshall because it has excellent horse trails and is large enough that hunters can usually locate an isolated basin and have it all to themselves.

3.) In the southwestern area, the mountains south and west of Darby on U.S. 93 in Ravalli County which comprises the Montana half of the Selway-Bitterroot Wilderness Area are an excellent elk hunting Spot. This is roadless country, and the terrain is steep.

4.) In central Montana, the Big Belt and Little Belt mountains east of Helena on U.S. 91 in Lewis & Clark County provide big bulls every year. The Augusta area near of Wolf Creek is especially good.

5.) In southcentral Montana, the entire Gallatin River drainage south of Belgrade on U.S. 191 in Gallatin County is excellent for trophy bulls, as is the Yellowstone River drainage to the east. These twin drainages receive a large flow of migrating Yellowstone elk in late fall, and many huge bulls are harvested every fall and winter. A special late season elk hunt is offered in these drainages just outside Yellowstone Park each winter to harvest the elk that migrate out of Yellowstone. A hunter who can not get away in the fall might find this December/January hunt appealing. Many huge bulls are killed during this hunt, which requires a special permit, but it is not too difficult to be drawn for one.

6.) In the southwestern part of the state, the Madison and Jefferson river drainages north and south of Ennis on U.S. 287 in Madison County are top elk producers.

7.) In the southwest, the Anaconda-Pintler Wilderness Area north of Wisdom in the Big Hole River drainage is excellent for trophy bull elk.

New Mexico

The best elk hunting is found in northern New Mexico in the high rugged mountains of the Continental Divide. Several huge private ranches and Indian reservations allow controlled hunting for elk and are fast gaining a reputation for providing record book trophy hunting.

1.) In the north, one of the best public hunting areas is in the north and central part of Rio Arriba County south of Chama on U.S. 84. Another good spot in this area extends from Chama due east into Taos County to just west of the Rio Grande River.

2.) In the northern part of the state, six state-owned Fish & Wildlife Areas (units 4 and 55) are tops for elk. They are the Humphries, Sargent, Uracca, Valle Vidal, and Colin Neblet north and south. The Valle Vidal area has been averaging a 5-point or better bull harvest in recent years.

3.) Some of the best hunting in the state is in the Carson and Santa Fe National Forests. Top spots are the area surrounding Chama on U.S. 84 in Rio Arriba County, and the area around Tres Piedras on U.S. 85 west of Taos County.

4.) In the northern part of the state, The Carson National Forest near Questa and the Red River drainage east of Tres Piedras on state route 38 is good for big bulls. The Pecos area at the south end of the Santa Fe National Forest, east of the city of Santa Fe, is also good for elk. In addition, Taos and the Eagles Nest area to the north produce some nice bulls.

5.) The Jicarilla Indian Reservation, headquartered out of Dulce, offers exclusive fee trophy bull elk hunting. This reservation is one of the best private elk hunting areas in the West for trophy bull elk.

6.) Another excellent private trophy hunting enterprise is the vast Moreno Ranch in northern New Mexico. This 50,000 acre ranch boasts a harvest record of 68% bulls which went 5x5 or better. Another private ranch which offers exclusive trophy bull elk hunting is the Vermejo Park Cattle Ranch.

Oregon

The vast majority of elk in Oregon are found in the Oregon Coast Mountains and the west slopes of the Cascade Mountains. The northeast corner of the state also has good elk hunting in the Blue Mountains, along with the extreme eastern part of the state along the Idaho border. There are lots of elk in Oregon, but underbrush is heavy where most elk are located in the western rain forests. Add to that the fact that hunting pressure is often intense, and you have some difficult hunting conditions.

1.) In the northern Coast Mountains, one of the best elk hunting areas is in the Wilson River drainage east of U.S. 101 in Tillamook County, and the Saddle Mountain area near Trask.

2.) The best southern Coast Mountain areas are in the mountains surrounding Eugene in Lane County. Another good area is the Coos River drainage east of Coos Bay on U.S. 101 in Coos County. The McKenzie River drainage east of Vida on U.S. 126 in Lane County is also good elk hunting, as is the North Umpqua River drainage east of Roseburg on I-5 in Douglas County of the Siskyou National Forest.

3.) In the northeast corner of the state, the Eagle Cap Wilderness Area is excellent for elk hunting. This area is in the Blue Mountains of the Wallowa-Whitman National Forest. Best spots are the Minam, Lostine, and Imnaha rivers, as well as Eagle, Bear, and Big creeks. South of Wallowa in Wallowa County, another good spot in this area is the La Grande area on U.S. 30 in Union County, especially in the La Grande River drainage to the north.

4.) In the far eastern part of the state, the Hell's Canyon National Recreation Area along the Idaho border is a good producer of bull elk. This rugged area is accessible from state route 82 east to Enterprise, where the U.S. Forest Service has a recreation headquarters.

Washington

Washington has a large elk herd, but it also has a lot of hunters in the field pursuing them, and sometimes the pressure gets intense in this populous state. Either/or hunting is now required, meaning you must choose to hunt with bow during archery season or gun during rifle season, but you cannot do both in one season.

1.) In the southcentral part of the state, the Yakima region is the biggest producer of elk. The top areas are unit 356 (Bumping), 358 (Bumping-Bethel), 360 (Bethel), and 328 (Naneum).

2.) Excellent elk densities are found in the far west coastal region from the strait of Juan De Fuca all the way south to the Columbia River. The two top elk producers are unit 615 near Clearwater on U.S. 101 in Jefferson County just southwest of Olympic National Park, and unit 618 near Methany.

3.) Good elk hunting is found in the Mount St. Helens region on the west slopes of the Cascades. Some of the best drainages for elk are the Cowlitz, Toutle, and Lewis rivers in Lewis and Cowlitz counties east of Columbia Heights on I-5. Other good areas in this region are unit-516 near Packwood on U.S. 14 in the upper Cowlitz River drainage, and unit-560 in the upper Lewis River drainage southeast of Spirit Lake.

4.) In the southeast, the Spokane region is located in the Blue Mountains. Unlike much of Washington's elk habitat, there is less brush in this area, and consequently hunters see more elk. In fact, this relatively small area has a harvest comparable to other regions that are much larger. The best areas are unit-169 near Wenaha and unit-175 at Lickcreek.

5.) The Sound region covers the western slopes of the Cascades from the Canadian border down to the southwest corner of Mt. Rainier National Park. The best elk hunting area is in unit-472 in the White River drainage east of Enumclaw on U.S. 410 in King County. Another good area is in unit-418 in the upper Nooksack River drainage northeast of Bellingham on I-5 in Whatcom County just below the Canadian border.

Wyoming

The major elk populations are in the northwestern part of the state south and east of Yellowstone National Park, and in the northcentral area in the Bighorn National Forest. The top elk producing areas are in the Teton National Forest south of Yellowstone Park, and the Bridger National Forest southeast of Jackson in the western part of the state.

1.) Two major drainages in the Teton National Forest account for about one-third of the total elk harvest in Wyoming. They are the Gros Ventre and Hoback river drainages in northwestern Wyoming south of the park. The Gros Ventre River drainage east of Kelley on U.S. 191 in Teton County is the top elk producing area in the state. The Hoback drainage nearly matches the Gros Ventre in total elk kill. It is located southeast of Jackson on U.S. 191 in Teton County.

2.) In the southwestern part of the state, some of the largest concentrations of bull elk are found in the Absaroka Mountains east of Yellowstone National Park and west of Cody on both sides of U.S. 14-20. Besides harboring a large resident elk herd, the Absaroka Mountains also accommodate a large migrating elk herd from Yellowstone Park each fall. The best areas are near peaks such as Castle, Cathedral, Silvertip, Sunlight, and Moose. The Manaco Camp up the craggy canyons of Moose Mountain is especially good.

3.) In the western part of the state, the Wyoming Mountain Range of the Bridger National Forest is often overlooked, but offers excellent elk hunting. This area extends between Alpine Junction on U.S. 89 in Sublette County to La Barge on U.S. 189. Specifically, try Grayback Ridge, plus Cliff and La Barge creeks near Fontenelle Lakes, and near Mt. Isabel to the south. Other good areas are the Little Greys drainage, the Deadmen Mountains, Blind Bull Canyon, and the heads of Grizzly and Cascade creeks.

4.) In the northcentral part of the state, the Bighorn National Forest is tops for elk hunting, especially in the mountains around Burgess on U.S. 14 in Sheridan County.

5.) In the southcentral part of Wyoming, the Medicine Bow National Forest west of Albany on state route 10 in Carbon County is very good elk hunting. Specifically, try the area around Saratoga Springs east of Wislope on state route 130.

Appendix C

ADDRESSES OF KEY INFORMATION SOURCES

The following list of addresses covers four areas: state wildlife agencies, regional U.S. Forest Service offices, western topographical map source, and the Rocky Mountain Elk Foundation. Use the first three to pinpoint a specific elk hunting area, and the last to support and better understand the elk.

State Wildlife Agencies

Arizona Game And Fish Department
2222 W. Greenway Road
Phoenix, Arizona 85023
(602) 942-3000

Colorado Division Of Wildlife
6060 Broadway
Denver, Colorado 85023
(303) 297-1192

Idaho Fish And Game Department
600 S. Walnut Street
Boise, Idaho 83707
(208) 334-3700

Montana Dept. Of Fish, Wildlife, Parks
1420 East Sixth Avenue
Helena, Montana 59601
(406) 449-2535

New Mexico Game And Fish Department
Villagre Building
Santa Fe, New Mexico 87503
(505) 827-2923

Oregon Dept. Of Fish And Wildlife
P.O. Box 3503
Portland, Oregon 97208
(503) 229-5551

Washington Dept. of Game
600 N. Capital Way
Olympia, Washington 98504
(206) 753-5700

Wyoming Game And Fish Department
Cheyenne, Wyoming 82002
(307) 777-763

U.S. Forest Service

Below are the regional offices of the U.S. Forest Service. You can obtain specific information and maps from them for a particular National Forest.

Region 1 (Montana, Northern Idaho)
Federal Building
Missoula, Montana 59807
(406) 329-3316

Region 2 (Colorado, Part of Wyoming)
11177 W. 8th Avenue
P.O. Box 25127
Lakewood, Colorado 80225
(303) 234-3711

Region 3 (Arizona, New Mexico)
Federal Building
517 Gold Avenue S.W. Albuquerque, New Mexico 87102
(505) 766-2401

Region 4 (Nevada, Utah, Southern Idaho, Western Wyoming)
Federal Building
324 25th Street
Ogden, Utah 84401
(801) 626-3201

Region 6 (Oregon, Washington)
319 S.W. Pine Street
P.O. Box 3623
Portland, Oregon 97208
(503) 221-3625

Topographic Maps

First ask for free state order maps, locate your area, and then order the specific state, regional, county, or quadrangle maps to cover your hunting area.

U.S. Geological Survey
Branch of Distribution
Federal Center
Denver, Colorado 80225
(303) 234-3832

Rocky Mountain Elk Foundation

The Rocky Mountain Elk Foundation is a nonprofit organization dedicated to the cause of the elk. Membership includes a subscription to *Bugle* magazine, with elk info from cover to cover.

Rocky Mountain Elk Foundation
P.O.Box 8249
Missoula, Montana 59807
(800) 843-7633

Appendix D

SOURCES OF HUNTING INFORMATION

Below is a list of recommended books and videos to better prepare the prospective elk hunter for his upcoming western hunt. These can be ordered from Stoneydale Press Publishing Co., 205 Main Street, Drawer B, Stevensville, Montana 59870 1-800-237-7583

Books

1.) *Western Hunting Guide*, by Mike Lapinski
2.) *Successful Big Game Hunting*, by Duncan Gilchrist
3.) *Elk Hunting In The Northern Rockies*, by Ed Wolff
4.) *Montana Hunting Guide*, by Dale Burk
5.) *Bugling For Elk*, by Dwight Schuh
6.) *Complete Guide To Field Care Of Trophies*, by Duncan Gilchrist
7.) *Oregon Hunting Guide*, by John A. Johnson

Videos

1.) *Rocky Mountain Elk, Their Life Story*
2.) *Elk Hunting In The Rocky Mountain West*
3.) *Hunting Rocky Mountain Mule Deer*
4.) *Early Season Elk Hunting*
5.) *Planning Your Rocky Mountain Hunt*